insight text guide

Anica Boulanger-Mashberg

Così

Louis Nowra

insight®

▸innovative ▸engaging ▸evolving

First published in 2009. Reprinted 2010, 2012, 2015, 2016, 2017, 2018, 2020, 2021, 2024.

Insight Publications Pty Ltd
3/350 Charman Road
Cheltenham VIC 3192
Australia
Tel: +61 3 8571 4950
Email: books@insightpublications.com.au

www.insightpublications.com.au

National Library of Australia Cataloguing-in-Publication entry:

Boulanger-Mashberg, Anica.
Louis Nowra's Così : insight text guide / Anica Boulanger-Mashberg.
1st ed.
ISBN 9781921411045 (pbk.)
Insight text guide.
Bibliography.
For secondary school age.
Nowra, Louis, 1950–. Cosi.
A822.3

Other ISBNs:
9781925175073 (digital)

Cover design: The Modern Art Production Group

Proudly Printed in Australia by Ligare Book Printers.

contents

CHARACTER MAP

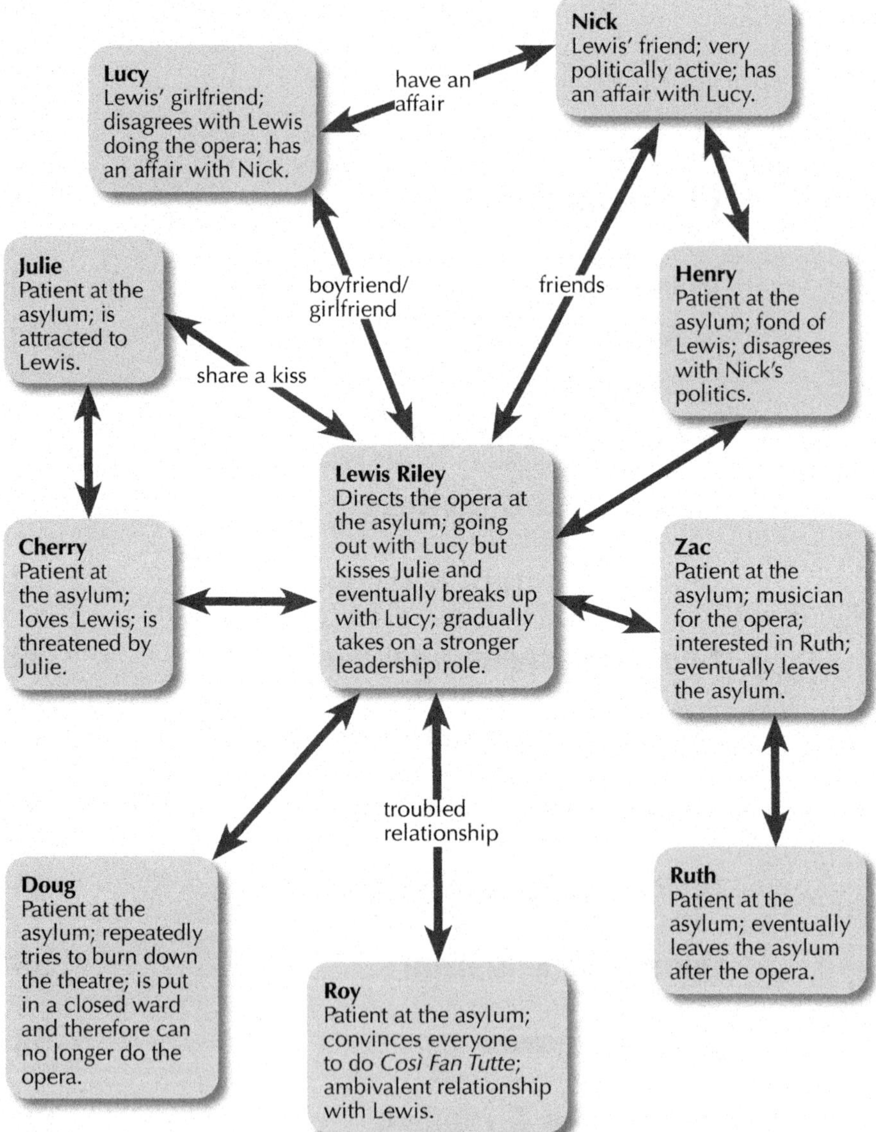

OVERVIEW

About the author

Louis Nowra was born in Melbourne in 1950 and lives in Australia. He is a prolific writer and has published works across many genres, including screenplays, radio plays, newspaper articles, translations, novels and autobiographies. He is probably best known, however, for his extensive body of work for the stage.

Early days

Nowra's childhood was not particularly happy, and his parents, who had a difficult relationship, often physically or emotionally abused him. His school life was a challenge too (although he enjoyed sports, particularly cricket) and was complicated by a severe head injury suffered in early adolescence, which for some time made concentration and communication difficult for him. He attended La Trobe University in Melbourne, and although he did not complete an undergraduate degree, he was awarded an Honorary Doctorate in 1996 from Griffith University, Queensland, in honour of his contributions to Australian literature.

The young Louis had connections with the theatre – one of his uncles was a stage manager – and his memoirs describe some of his first experiences with the stage. These early impressions influenced many of his plays.

Works

One of Nowra's first plays, *Kiss the One-Eyed Priest*, was produced in 1973 at La Mama, a Melbourne theatre with a tradition of supporting new Australian works. More than ten full-length plays followed, including *Inner Voices* (1977), *The Golden Age* (1985), *Summer of the Aliens* (1992), *Radiance* (1993), *The Incorruptible* (1995) and *Così* (1992). He wrote screenplays for the film versions of *Radiance* and *Così*, and also published two memoirs, *The Twelfth of Never* (1999) and *Shooting the Moon: A Memoir* (2004). His radio plays, many of which have been produced by ABC radio, include a version of *Summer of the Aliens*, later adapted for the stage.

Nowra has also written several novels, the most recent of which, *Ice* (2008), was shortlisted for the 2009 Miles Franklin Literary Award. Other awards include the Canada–Australia Literary Award (1993), a Logie for Most Outstanding Documentary in 2009 for the television series *First Australians* (co-written with Rachel Perkins and Beck Cole) and the 1994 Victorian Premier's Literary Award for his play *The Temple*. He has also won several awards for *Così*, including the Play Award in the 1992 NSW Premier's Literary Awards, and an AFI Award in 1996 for Best Adapted Screenplay. Nowra's broad writing experience also encompasses a number of collaborations with composers (including Sarah de Jong, his first wife), film directors and other screenwriters.

Nowra's works cover a broad range of eras and geographical and social settings, including Russia, historical Latin America and contemporary Sarajevo. Alongside these international settings, Nowra also regularly sets his works in Australia, and several of his works, including *Radiance*, are concerned with the experiences of Indigenous Australians. A theme common in much of Nowra's work is the idea of outsiders: *Così*, like another of his best-known plays, *The Golden Age*, presents characters that are outcasts from society and damaged human beings. In *Così*, this is very blatant: the patients in the asylum are obviously individuals who don't fit into the outside world. However, within the asylum and the opera production they develop a sense of purpose and community.

Nowra also worked as a director and a drama teacher, and had an extremely brief career as an actor when he stepped in at short notice to play the role of the narrator in a production of *Summer of the Aliens*. Apparently, everyone thought he'd be better off if he concentrated on writing.

Synopsis

(Note: for the purposes of this guide Mozart's opera will always be referred to as *Così Fan Tutte*, and the shorter title, *Così*, will refer to Nowra's play. The only exception will be when quoting the text directly, where the characters may call the opera *Così*.)

Set in 1971 in a burnt-out theatre adjoining a mental institution in Melbourne, *Così* is the story of an unconventional production of Mozart's opera *Così Fan Tutte*. Lewis, a recent university graduate, finds himself employed to direct a play with a group of patients in a mental institution. Lewis' university education has not prepared him for such a demanding task, a challenge increased by the explosive blend of personalities within the group. The characters' relationships are the basis for the tensions and conflicts of the play, but are also responsible for much of *Così*'s humour.

On arriving at the asylum, Lewis meets the patients who have 'volunteered' to participate (some more willingly than others). The company comprises Zac, a musician who is usually heavily drugged; Doug, whose high energy and unreserved interpersonal style is coupled with an unhealthy fascination with fire; Henry, whose shyness is balanced by his passion for Australia's military history; Cherry, a jealousy-prone, sex-obsessed live wire; Ruth, anxious and relentlessly rational with obsessive tendencies; and Julie, a hairdresser with a drug dependency. And then there's Roy.

Roy, the group's natural leader, has his heart set on producing *Così Fan Tutte*: an opera he adores and that he believes is endowed with the power to make the whole world more beautiful. Roy has trouble convincing Lewis and the others that *Così* (as he affectionately calls it) has any value at all: they think it old-fashioned, dull and irrelevant. And besides, nobody in the group speaks Italian, and many can barely sing. For Roy, these obstacles are merely challenges, and it is his determination and passion (sometimes misplaced, engendering frustration in the others), which drive the rehearsals. Often in conflict with Lewis over the progress of the show, Roy has a tendency to make his criticisms very personal, not just aiming them at Lewis' directing skills, but also discrediting his character.

The production faces many setbacks, including Doug's arson attempt on the theatre (and his subsequent admission to the closed ward) and Roy's paralysing attack of stage fright, but the process of overcoming these trials strengthens the participants as individuals and as a group. When Doug is confined to the closed ward, Lewis reluctantly steps into the role of Ferrando and begins to genuinely commit to the production (to the exclusion of other aspects of his life). The production began as an 'experiment' (p.22) which was intended to bring the patients 'out of their shells' (p.6), but in the end, it is perhaps Lewis who comes out of his shell the most.

During the rehearsal period, we also meet Lucy and Nick, Lewis' girlfriend and best friend, who represent the world outside the asylum. As the patients and the opera gradually become Lewis' main concern, Lucy and Nick continue their protests against the Vietnam War and their fight against capitalism: convictions once shared by all three. Lewis' shifting priorities are a source of conflict between the friends and, as Lucy and Lewis drift further apart, Lucy grows closer to Nick. Nick and Lucy, who think that Lewis has sold out on them, eventually reveal that they've been having an affair.

At the conclusion of the play, *Così Fan Tutte* is finally performed. Lewis farewells his cast; delivers a monologue to the audience, informing us about what happens to the characters of *Così* in the future; and then turns out the lights in the theatre – a symbolic as well as a practical close to the narrative.

Character summaries

Lewis Riley

Central character; fresh from university; not very confident; comes to the asylum to work with the patients. Lives with his girlfriend, Lucy (and their friend Nick), but shares a kiss with Julie (a patient). Becomes more confident through the opera, rises to the challenge, and eventually chooses the production over Lucy and a life of student politics.

Roy

Central character; patient in the asylum; driving force behind the production of *Così Fan Tutte*. Grew up in orphanages and with foster parents, but has constructed a fictional childhood of joy and high culture. Swings wildly between moods of excitement and depression. Roy is passionate but his blind and unrealistic dreams of greatness alienate him from the others.

Doug

Brazen and confident; high-energy; constantly challenging others, either physically or by confronting them verbally or emotionally. Has a history of pyromania and a disturbed relationship with his mother. Doug is resistant to participating in the opera, but keen to be a part of the group, if only to stir things up.

Henry

Once a lawyer; once married; now a long-term resident in institutions. Painfully shy, Henry has an almost debilitating stutter and a paralysed arm (eventually revealed to be of psychological rather than physiological origin). He is preoccupied with military history and memories of his parents. Physically strong; violent when he becomes angry; protective of Lewis, for whom he slowly develops a quiet affection.

Julie

Short-term patient in the asylum due to drug dependency. Sees life in terms of drugs; loves the opera because it gets her out of the oppressive ward and makes her feel alive – like drugs. She is attracted to Lewis (they kiss) but eventually confesses that she has a girlfriend to whom she is returning when she leaves.

Cherry

Has been in institutions for some time; has aggressive, violent tendencies – especially when she feels her affections have been thwarted. Preoccupied with food and with sex; jealous of Lewis and Julie's relationship. She is the only patient who really stands up to Roy.

Zac

Musician; often heavily drugged and sometimes in and out of consciousness during rehearsals. Thinks Mozart's music is boneless and would rather be doing Wagner. Preoccupied with sex and tries to proposition Ruth.

Ruth

An obsessive woman who lacks confidence and has anxiety issues; has been in violent relationships. Ruth struggles to comprehend differences between reality, illusion and pretending. Eventually stands up for herself against Zac.

Lucy

Lives with Lewis, her boyfriend, and their friend Nick. She is a university student, a passionate protester against the Vietnam War, and a fighter for social justice. Has an affair with Nick and breaks up with Lewis.

Nick

Lewis' friend; lives with Lewis and Lucy. Passionate supporter of communists in Vietnam, and protester against the war. Also a director of theatre he feels is socially worthy (like Brecht). Is insensitive towards the patients, treating them as clichéd 'crazy' people; has an affair with Lucy.

Justin

Incidental character; social worker responsible for setting up the theatre project. Introduces Lewis to the patients, and gives Lewis (and the audience) some simplistic pointers on how to handle the patients and the situation.

BACKGROUND & CONTEXT

Publication and production history

Così was first performed in April 1992 by Sydney's Company B at the Belvoir Street Theatre. Following this production, Nowra made revisions to the text: most notably, removing or re-writing the domestic scenes (of Lewis' life beyond the rehearsals) so that the entire play takes place within the asylum, specifically the theatre. This revised script, published by Currency Press in 1994, remains the standard script for publication and production.

In 1996 a film version of *Così* was released, with Nowra adapting his own script as a screenplay. While the film tells essentially the same story as the stage play (Lewis overcoming various, often comical, trials in the process of readying the asylum cast for its operatic debut), there were many changes made for the film version of the script. Some of these were suggested or required by Miramax, the American company that financed half of the film. (More discussion of the film version may be found in the 'Different interpretations' section of this guide.)

Louis and Lewis

Così is the second in a trilogy of plays Nowra intended to write, a semi-autobiographical series. The first of these was *Summer of the Aliens,* in which the teenaged character Lewis represents the teenaged Louis Nowra at a period of his life when he felt so disconnected from adults that he imagined they might actually have been colonised by aliens. The narrator in this play represents an older Lewis looking back at his youth (just as the writer, Louis, was looking back). It must have been particularly odd for Nowra to perform this role in a 1992 Melbourne Theatre Company production, playing a version of himself simultaneously watching a younger actor in yet another version of himself!

In *Così*, years have passed and Lewis is now a fresh university graduate, unsure of himself in the world and again facing people who are somewhat 'alien' to him – the patients in the institution. The story of the young director working with a group of people with various mental disturbances comes directly from Louis' life: in the late 1960s Nowra worked at a mental institution and was involved with adapting and producing a Gilbert and Sullivan opera with some of the patients.

But despite the blatant reference of the similarity of names, Lewis and Louis are not identical. Audiences are invited to draw parallels between character and writer, but are also warned to maintain separation. In his introduction to the Currency Press edition of *Summer of the Aliens*, Nowra describes the writing as a 'black hole of fiction, surrounded by a halo of truth' (p.vi), and this could describe *Così* too.

The intended final play in this trilogy is yet to emerge.

Historical setting

Così was written in the 1990s but is set in the early 1970s. While the entire play takes place in the sheltered and enclosed space of the theatre adjoining the asylum, the social era provides an important background for the dynamics within the institution. The 1970s was a decade of great social change, both in Australia and in other parts of the world. In *Così*, characters like Doug and Julie allude to some of the social phenomena that represent the changing values a young person like Lewis faced in transition to adulthood. Some of the things Doug discusses, like 'free love' (p.18, p.85, p.86), rock and roll and the phrase 'make love, not war' (p.15, p.72), are notions that have become clichés of a contemporary idea of the 1970s.

The Vietnam War, against which Nick and Lucy are passionate protesters, was a war that divided Australians. Nick and Lucy represent the mostly young, left-wing activists who rebelled against the official military commitment of their country by supporting the Viet Cong (communists) in Vietnam. As Nick explains in the play, the aim was to defend North Vietnam against American imperialism with both moral and financial aid.

The 1970s was also a period when Australians were evaluating their place in the world, their allegiances and beliefs, and their relationships with a global society. This can be seen in Lewis' fluctuations between protesting against the American involvement in Vietnam and wanting to support Australian 'culture', even if that might mean producing a European opera inside a mental institution. Lewis' youthful and developing sense of self and his priorities parallel a certain sense of 'coming-of-age' that was occurring culturally in Australia during this period.

Mozart's *Così*

Mozart's work *Così Fan Tutte* (1790) is one of many operas Mozart wrote in the late 1700s. The Italian libretto is by Lorenzo da Ponte, with whom Mozart had previously worked on several other operas. The title, difficult to translate directly into English, means roughly 'thus they all do', but is generally interpreted as 'all women are like that'.

The opera, for six singers and a chorus, is about fidelity and love between the sexes. The characters are Dorabella and Fiordiligi (the women), Ferrando and Guglielmo (soldiers; the women's respective lovers), Despina (the women's handmaid) and Don Alfonso (an old philosopher). The basic premise (as Roy describes in the first scene of *Così*) is that the men decide to put the women's faithfulness to the test by disguising themselves and attempting to court each other's lover. Don Alfonso and Despina encourage and direct the men and women's behaviour, orchestrating much of the action. The men find their trust misplaced and the women unfaithful – each falling for the other's lover – but because it is a comic opera, all is resolved happily.

A note on the psychological terminology

It is important to maintain sensitivity when writing about the characters in *Così*. Characters in the play sometimes refer to each other in ways that it would be inappropriate for us, an audience, to describe them. Nick, for example, calls the patients a group of 'madmen' (p.1), 'nuts' (p.47) and 'loonies' (p.77). Lucy calls them 'mad people' (p.70). The patients are even more verbally aggressive, and often call each other names that are patently unacceptable and clearly intended as abuse. For example, Roy calls Henry 'a failure' (p.27) and says that 'psychopath is too kind a word to describe' Doug (p.9); Cherry calls Julie 'a junkie' and a 'head shrinker' – slang for being sexually promiscuous with the institution's staff (p.40); Doug calls Julie 'a looney and a junkie' (p.72) and Cherry a 'fat dog' (p.86). Clearly these are insults traded between the patients, and should not be adopted when writing about the characters.

Justin, the social worker, makes an effort to explain to Lewis that the patients are simply 'normal people who have done extraordinary things, thought extraordinary thoughts' (p.5). Justin's description is an important reminder to an audience not to make assumptions, and not to stereotype or judge the characters just because they are in an asylum. This is a difficult balance to maintain, because in many cases the humour of the play comes from the characters' bizarre, unbalanced and uninhibited behaviour.

GENRE, STRUCTURE & LANGUAGE

Genre

Despite the seriousness of its underlying subject matter (mental illness), *Così* is a comedy. It is also a contemporary script that favours realism and naturalism over other more symbolic or spectacle-based forms. Many of the conversations and behaviours are extreme and 'over the top', but this is consistent with the characters themselves, and stylistically they are still presented in a very naturalistic way rather than being heightened or exaggerated. With the exception of Lewis' closing monologue, the naturalistic conventions of the 'fourth wall' are maintained – the characters do not break out of their 'realities' to acknowledge or communicate with the audience.

Black comedy

Così is an example of black comedy, a theatrical form that allows serious or sensitive issues to be presented in a comical context. In a black comedy, the audience is encouraged to laugh at things that are not normally considered humorous. Examples of 'serious' issues that are dealt with in black comedy include misfortunes, confusions, danger and even death. However, black comedy is not usually graphic, shocking or confronting; these are elements of other theatrical styles. Black comedies are not about 'making fun' of anyone or anything, but about exploring meaningful issues in accessible and entertaining ways.

Often in black comedy the juxtaposition (placing of different things beside each other) of the sensitive content with the amusing context helps the audience to become more aware of the underlying serious issue. For example, in *Così*, one of the amusing recurring lines is 'go burn a cat'. This insult is based on the incident Doug describes when he 'accidentally' burnt his mother's house (pp.19–20). The incident itself is not amusing if taken out of context. Pyromania, a condition in which individuals have a fascination with fire and difficulty controlling their impulses to start fires, is dangerous and serious. But within the context of the play, Doug's story is entertaining and amusing. It is punctuated by comical observations such as 'there's no such thing as grace under pressure for a burning cat' (p.20), and the audience is encouraged to laugh at the story while empathising with Lewis' discomfort and sense of apprehension about working with Doug.

In a black comedy, the central characters rarely 'grow' or change along their journey. In other theatrical forms, central characters learn from the conflicts and challenges that they encounter in the course of the play. But in a black comedy, it is common for the characters to reach the end of the play without displaying any significant growth or change in their personalities. Even Lewis' growth is subtle: Lucy says accusingly to him, 'working with these people has changed you' (p.70), but there is not much evidence of this. His final monologue gives no hint of how his life has changed as a result of his experiences with the opera. All he says is that 'by the following year' he happens to find himself in Sydney (p.89). There is no sense that he is a different person or has significantly learnt from his time working with the patients. He has come out of his shell (as the project intended for the patients), and gained some confidence in himself, but he has not significantly *changed*.

Similarly, some of the patients grow subtly throughout the play – for example, the shy, reluctant Henry of the first scene becomes a loyal and active cast member who even sings. In his final monologue, Lewis hints that the only ones who have really made progress with their lives are two of the more minor characters: Ruth, who has 'left the institution to become a time and motion expert', turning her obsessions into a useful and productive talent; and Zac, who starts several bands, playing the music he enjoyed more than Mozart all along (p.89). The others appear to continue their lives as before – Roy stays in the institution; Nick and Lucy continue on the career paths they were on at the beginning of the play; Cherry and Doug are only briefly mentioned and seem unchanged. Sadly, Henry and Julie both die.

Structure

Così, like Mozart's *Così Fan Tutte*, is structured in two acts, which are further divided into scenes. The scenes in the first act average about 12 pages of dialogue, and those in the second act are slightly shorter. The play is roughly divided in half by the two acts (often the place for an interval), with the second act slightly shorter than the first. The scenes all take place in chronological order.

All of the scenes occur within the theatre, and this, combined with the naturalistic chronology, contributes to the sense of long-term routine and confinement that characterises many of the patients' experiences in the institution. As Cherry and Julie both note, one of the most exciting things about the opera is that it gets the patients out of their wards and gives them a change of scenery, a focus and a purpose to their everyday reality. Cherry is excited about eating lunch in the theatre instead of the ward (p.20), and Julie similarly finds that rehearsing the opera gives her an escape from the ward, and something to distract her from the mundaneness of being in the institution (p.36).

Language

Style of dialogue

As might be expected from the naturalistic style of the play, the characters use contemporary Australian everyday language, which, for the patients, often includes slang and swearing. (Doug is the most notorious example of this, habitually swearing to add emphasis to his speech, and self-consciously using explicit language to deliberately upset, shock or provoke people.) The dialogue is not overly symbolic or rich in terms of imagery, metaphor or dramatic irony. It tends to be concrete and descriptive, describing characters' feelings about their lives and their experiences with the opera.

There are some exceptions. Examples include Roy's very poetic description of his imagined childhood (pp.63–4); Lucy's persuasive philosophical arguments against love (p.70) and Julie's vivid descriptions of how drugs make her see the world (p.32, p.37). These moments make use of more figurative language, such as Roy's constructed memories of 'servants dancing on fingertips' (p.64), or Julie's phrases 'like lying in a warm, cloudy river' and 'felt like mercury' (p.37). These more heightened uses of language are an indication of the characters' states of mind – they describe moments in the characters' lives that were somehow unreal or magical.

In stark contrast, characters like Henry and Ruth relate painful and apparently truthful memories of their past in very blunt, literal, pragmatic language. For example, Ruth (under the protective cover of darkness during the power outage) details an abusive relationship she was once in. Her vocabulary is harsh and matter of fact as she describes how she 'slashed his car tyres' (p.66).

Distinguishing characters by language use

The differences in the kind of language used by each character are subtle. They all share a broad social and historical context, which is reflected in their use of similar vocabulary and rhythms of speech. The patients (and gradually Lewis) also share the context of the asylum, and this influences their speech habits too – for example, they often repeat the same insults.

However, Nowra does use language to help distinguish between characters. For example, Doug is crude and blunt in the way he speaks, especially to Lewis. He swears; speaks in short, sharp sentences; and often uses slang. A good example is his first conversation with Lewis, where he asks a series of brief, frank questions, like 'shacked up with a few sheilas, are you?' (p.6). This style of speech contrasts with that of some of the other characters. For example, Julie tends to speak more formally, in longer, more complex sentences; Ruth is very precise, concrete and detailed when she speaks; Cherry is emotional, passionate and forceful; and Lewis, at least for the first half of the play, tends to be polite, careful and even apologetic.

Q Which characters do you think the following lines belong to, and why? (Think about the vocabulary, the rhythms, and the tone of speech. You can check your answers by looking up the page numbers and finding the lines.)

- 'I wonder, Zac, if you could practise outside? (p.31)
- 'Most women fight hard to keep men out of their pants.' (p.61)
- 'Christ ... better piss off out the back.' (p.72)

SCENE-BY-SCENE ANALYSIS

Act One, Scene One (pp.1–13)

Summary: *Lewis enters the asylum for the first time, accompanied by Lucy and Nick; Justin introduces the patients (except Zac, who arrives late); Roy proposes* Così *as the project for the group; we glimpse how each character relates to Lewis and to the project.*

The opening scene in the play is a very practical one: it introduces us to Lewis and his role in the play; to each of the patients; and to Mozart's *Così Fan Tutte*, which is such an important element of the text that it is almost a character in itself. As the play progresses, we see how each character relates to the opera, and what these relationships represent about the characters. The other important introduction in this scene is to the theatre, as both the physical setting for the play, and also as a symbolic space for the narrative to inhabit. The first moments of the play take place in darkness. This is symbolic on many levels, and the first few lines of dialogue give us a large amount of information very quickly.

The darkness represents the nature of the theatre and of performance: until a theatrical work has been rehearsed and put together, it is nothing but an idea and there is no light, no sound, no spectacle. At this moment, all that exists (both for us and for Lewis) is the *possibility* of a play. So far, there is no 'magic' of theatre. We are at the very beginning, without even light to make the moment come alive. Similarly, the darkness represents Lewis' lack of knowledge, preparedness and inspiration for the task at hand. He is very much 'in the dark' about what to expect from the patients, and from his role working with them.

Note, however, that the initial stage direction indicates that as the door opens 'a chink of daylight enters' – perhaps this is symbolic of Lewis bringing with him a tiny glimmer of the outside world that will touch the inmates. He steps from the known outside world (which the stage direction tells us is full of daylight, representing the safe familiarity of Lewis' life) and enters this symbolically 'dark' space with two friends from his world outside the institution. Lucy and Nick, who are not really able to help him, here represent Lewis' knowledge and experience from the 'outside' world. They leave him alone there, only a page later, just as his previous experience and his expectations of this event abandon him.

Although Lewis is the central character, he is so lacking in confidence here that the first line is not his, but Lucy's. She asks 'where are the lights?' (p.1), which not only is exactly what the audience is wondering, but also is typical of Lucy's personality – she is practical, to the point, and questions the social value of the kind of theatre in which Lewis is interested. Lewis' reply – 'don't know' – similarly tells us a lot about Lewis (p.1). Not only has he landed himself in a situation of which he is not, on a practical level, in control, but he is also not in control on a motivational, inspirational, creative level: he can't even begin to imagine how he might turn on the symbolic 'lights' for the patients at the asylum. He has no idea how he will bring their theatre alive. This is confirmed later in the stage direction: '*There is a long silence … Lewis … doesn't know where to begin*' (p.7). Luckily, Lucy finds the light switch for him just before she leaves, but not before Roy has broken into the theatre.

Roy is Lewis' first interaction with the world he is about to inhabit for the rest of the play, and it is fitting that Roy is the first patient Lewis meets, as Roy is the one most passionate about *Così Fan Tutte*, and the one who drives the narrative. In fact, the symbolism of the dark theatre is closely linked to Roy too – Lucy is unable to find the light switch until Roy enters. This indicates that Roy is really the life of the show, the (sometimes misdirected) energy of the asylum and the centre of *Così*.

Justin follows closely behind Roy, introducing each new character to Lewis (although he leaves before Zac arrives).

Key point

When it comes to thinking about the patients, Justin offers Lewis (and the audience) an alternative to Nick's insensitive and knee-jerk labelling of them as 'madmen' (p.1). Justin's suggestions are to think of them as 'normal people who have done extraordinary things, thought extraordinary thoughts' (p.5), and, perhaps less helpfully, 'a madman is someone who arrives at a fancy dress party dressed in the Emperor's new clothes' (p.7). These examples show the difficulty of classifying the patients, remaining politically correct and sensitive, and finding ways to relate to them.

Lewis' first meeting with each of the other patients, as with Roy, provides a good indication of how his relationship with the character will proceed. In Doug's first conversation, he challenges and questions Lewis' role as director, and also attempts to offend Lewis and incite a reaction by asking whether Lewis is a 'poofter' (p.4). This characterises their ongoing relationship, with Doug continually challenging Lewis. Lewis' first interaction with Henry is Henry's refusal to shake Lewis' hand; this sets the tone for Henry's shyness and reluctance to embrace the situation (although he eventually overcomes this). Cherry, from her first entrance, is confident, defensive, confrontational and cynical about the opera, claiming that it is 'just another thing about the battle of the sexes' (p.11). Julie is quiet and reserved, not rising to Doug's attempt to provoke her (p.7), and her only lines are to introduce herself (p.7) and to express her support for the opera: 'I prefer this to the ward' (p.12). Ruth's first interaction, typically, is to question the essential truth and 'reality' of what will happen on stage. She enquires earnestly and anxiously about how they will manage to have cappuccinos on stage (p.10), expresses concerns about her abilities, and seeks reassurance from Lewis. Finally, Zac enters late, and leaves a moment later: a sign of his somewhat detached involvement with the opera as a whole. This detachment is due partly to his persistent state of overmedicated stupor, and partly to his dislike for Mozart's music.

In this first scene, we also 'meet' *Così Fan Tutte*, both practically, in Roy's plot synopsis of the opera (p.9), and also in terms of what it represents for Roy, and will eventually represent for the others to varying degrees. Roy calls *Così* 'the greatest opera in the whole world' (p.8). But already the opera has caused conflict and chaos for the patients, as they argue not only about its social and moral value but also about whether or not they can achieve a performance of it. Roy passionately claims that 'the music of this opera keeps the world in harmony' (p.13). It will be up to the rest of the play to refute or support this claim.

Key point

Justin says that the point of the theatre project is to give the patients something to do, to 'keep them interested' and 'bring them out of their shells' (p.6). This is an important statement to return to later in the text, to question whether the opera does bring them – and, indeed, Lewis – out of their shells.

Key vocabulary

Jerry Lewis and Dean Martin: comedy duo in America in the 1950s.

Moratorium: generally describes an agreed delay or suspension of a particular activity. In this case, it refers to the protest Nick is organising against the Vietnam War. Several such demonstrations took place in Melbourne in the early 1970s.

Q How does this scene set up parallels between 'madness' and theatre?

Q How do the different characters define 'truth' and 'reality' in this scene? (Think about direct observations about truth, like Ruth's, but also less literal expressions of 'truth' – for example, for Roy the opera represents a form of escapism where he can define his own 'truth'.)

Act One, Scene Two (pp.13–22)

Summary: *Lewis finishes the auditions and they debate whether it is really possible to do the opera; the patients eat lunch outside while Lewis listens to Nick on the radio discussing the moratorium; Doug tells Lewis the story about setting the cats on fire; Cherry tries to feed Lewis for the first time; Doug starts a fire in the toilets.*

In this scene we first get a sense of the magnitude of the task that is before Lewis. We can see from the auditions that, despite Roy's enthusiasm, his hand-picked cast is woefully ill-equipped to fulfil his dream of producing an Italian opera. Not only do none of them have opera training or speak Italian, some are barely able to speak at all. But Lewis is not prepared to give up yet and sends the patients out for lunch while he attempts to translate the libretto. This will be an ongoing pattern in the play: seemingly insurmountable challenges face the group, and yet are overcome each time.

There is also a glimpse of the 'outside' world, as Lewis listens to Nick on the radio. This 'real' world, the one beyond the asylum's theatre, will become progressively more distant and less important for Lewis as he engages more closely with the opera. Already, at this point, the outside world only exists for Lewis on the radio and not anywhere tangible. Lewis, frustrated by Nick's self-important idealism and hot passion to change the world, turns down the volume on the interview, actively lessening Nick's influence and refocusing his attention on the opera.

The characters' relationships with Lewis, their director, build on what we have seen in the previous scene. They tend to relate to Lewis in the way that they relate to authority. For example:

- Roy has a conflicting relationship both with Lewis and with authority, at once fawning and seeking approval yet also refusing to submit to decisions made by authority figures.
- Ruth is timid with Lewis and keen to get things right, presumably to avoid censure, although it is she who is judging herself.
- Doug refuses to compromise or modify his behaviour for Lewis' sake, is upfront and often aims to confront and shock.

Several characters in this scene have the opportunity to speak with Lewis alone, giving us a little more insight into their backgrounds. Doug's monologue about burning his mother's cats (pp.19–20) is the main example, and in the course of the discussion we learn a little more about Lewis as well as Doug, even though Lewis is hesitant to volunteer personal information.

At the end of this scene, Doug lights a fire in the toilets and a small kerfuffle erupts, contrasting with the calm, static conversations with Lewis just moments before. This is a reminder that chaos is never far away in the asylum and, by extension, in the outside world.

Q How does Doug's monologue employ the conventions of black comedy?

Q There are no stage directions for Lewis or Doug during Doug's long monologue (pp.19–20). Given what you already know about the characters, what kind of physical actions do you think might take place during this speech?

Act One, Scene Three (pp.22–35)

Summary: *Cherry unexpectedly takes the blame for Doug's arson attempt; Lewis joins in on the cover-up; Justin agrees to let the show continue; they begin rehearsing the first scene; we see Lewis and Julie alone together for the first time and sense their attraction; this is contrasted with Lewis and Cherry alone together.*

It is already clear that the opera has taken hold and drawn the group together. They each have reasons for wanting the rehearsals to continue – for example, Roy has his original dream to fulfil, and Cherry has her new crush, Lewis – but they are beginning to behave like a cast and an ensemble, caring about something larger than themselves. What Justin calls the 'experiment' (p.22) is beginning to work, despite the minor setback of Doug trying to set the toilets on fire! Justin had hoped to bring the patients out of their shells, but perhaps he wasn't prepared for the implications.

When Lewis joins the rest of the group in deceiving Justin about who really started the fire, he is breaking down a barrier between 'us' and 'them'; between the damaged and the un-damaged people; between the patients and the outside world. He shifts himself away from the world that Justin represents – a world where people try to help patients from the outside – to a position closer to equality with the patients, where he is part of the ensemble they are becoming. In contrast, Justin's comment, 'you're going out there a nobody and coming back a star' (p.24) – a common misquote from a line in the 1930s film *42nd Street* – shows how out of touch Justin is with what is actually going on in the asylum and in the rehearsals. It reveals how ready he is to turn to clichés in order to deal with the situation.

Key point

Justin gives us an important insight into the process and Lewis' experience when he says Lewis 'couldn't learn this at university. You know why, because it's about people!' (p.24). This is a key issue explored by the play: how people relate to each other, regardless of whether or not they are 'mad'.

A discussion with Ruth about truth, illusion and reality shows us how Lewis tries to modify his behaviour to deal with the differing needs of each of the patients, though he isn't always successful. Lewis tries to be sensitive to Ruth's need for constant reassurance about what is 'real' and what is an 'illusion', and he finally thinks he's figured out how to communicate with her on her own terms. Lewis instructs Ruth and Julie to stroll in the imaginary garden, and when Ruth asks 'what if we trip?' he replies 'all the rocks are an illusion, so you won't' (p.29). Ruth is only satisfied for a moment though, and then returns to her usual obsessions, counting how many steps she should take on stage.

Lewis' frustration with Ruth is then contrasted with his rational discussion with Julie while the others are outside for lunch. This is the first time Lewis and Julie have spoken properly, and they open up to each other. Lewis shares information about his relationship with Lucy and his previous experience with asylums (his grandmother's mental illness), and Julie discusses her thoughts on fidelity, and her experience in the asylum. This conversation, and the degree of ease with which they each discuss quite meaningful subjects, indicates the mutual attraction between them.

However, the calm conversation doesn't last long before first Cherry interrupts and then chaos breaks out again (this time offstage), as Doug has attempted to set fire to the theatre.

Key vocabulary

Bourgeois: referring to middle-class attitudes; generally used derisively.
Libretto: the 'book' or textual component of an opera.
Metaphysics: a branch of philosophy concerned with questions about reality, knowledge and being.

Q When Justin tries to call off the 'experiment', why does Lewis fight to keep the opera going (considering how challenging and frustrating it has been for him so far)?

Q What shifts can you identify in Lewis' language when he chats with Julie? How do these reflect how he feels about her? (Think about the pace of his dialogue as well as the content of his lines.)

Act One, Scene Four (pp.35–50)

Summary: *We discover Doug is back in the closed ward, putting a halt to the rehearsals; Roy emerges from his bout of depression with the inspired idea to cast Lewis in Doug's role; Nick arrives to offer assistance, and the patients are smitten with him until they discover his political preferences; Henry stands up for his father's honour, against Nick and the politics of the opera; Lewis reiterates his commitment to the opera, even above his commitment to Nick.*

This scene, the end of the first act and usually the last scene before the interval, is the emotional and dramatic climax of the text so far. The conflicts between characters reach their peak when Henry's anger finally overpowers his shyness and he attacks Nick both verbally and physically.

The scene begins with very low energy – Doug is back in the closed ward and no one can imagine how the opera can continue. Julie and Lewis are sharing another moment together when Cherry and Ruth arrive, both dealing with the latest trauma (Doug's arson attempt and his subsequent removal from the cast) in their habitual ways: Cherry tries her best to feed Lewis and to discourage his friendship with Julie, and Ruth has memorised every single line, cue and step in the opera. A conflict between Roy and Lewis is escalating until Roy has a brainwave – to cast Lewis in Doug's role – and they are back in familiar territory, with Roy passionate about the opera despite the obvious practical setbacks. Just as they are settling into this routine behaviour, Nick's arrival shakes everything up again.

For no apparent reason, all the patients seem instantly to like Nick and his direction, despite the fact that he is clearly nowhere near as sympathetic, patient or well-meaning as Lewis. Perhaps they are responding to Nick's decisiveness, or perhaps it is just the change in scenery, but suddenly they are all excited again, especially Roy. All is going well with the rehearsal until a discussion about the army costumes for the soldiers lets slip the fact that Nick (and, by extension, Lewis) supports the communists, and Henry can no longer control his reactions.

Henry's fury is grounded in his respect for his father, who fought in the war 'for you and ffffor me', he stutters angrily at Roy, and at the whole room (p.47). Once Henry finally speaks up it is as though a lifetime's worth of anger and frustration is unleashed, and, as the stage direction notes, '*anger repairs most of his stutter*' (p.46). Henry is so infuriated that he physically assails Nick, and '*grabs him in a bear hug*' (p.46). Nick responds self-assuredly to the outburst, calling the patients 'nuts', swearing at them, and leaving (p.47). Lewis is left to repair the damage within the group, attempting to placate Henry who is by this point beyond calming. The two of them reach an impasse when Henry attempts to leave and Lewis blocks his way: 'you'll have to hit me to get out' (p.49). The tension is very strong at this moment, as the patients (and the audience) wait to see what will happen. The situation is defused when Henry admits 'I don't want to hit you. I like you, you're not the Viet Cong' (p.49). A compromise, a resolution, even a kind of unity has been reached, and on this note the act concludes.

Key point

The moment when Lewis challenges Henry is the strongest moment in Lewis' behaviour so far. It is the first time Lewis really stands up to any of the patients, and, perhaps in the same way that they respected Nick for his decisiveness, the patients seem to have a new respect now for Lewis. He has shown them that at last he knows what he wants, and he will stand up for it if necessary. This is very different from his first, noncommittal, weak words at the beginning of the act.

Key vocabulary

American imperialism: used negatively here to refer to the Americans' attempt to extend their empire by exerting rule over foreign territories – here, Vietnam.

Communism: a political movement characterised by a faith in the rule of the state, and an aspiration towards a society without the divisions of class.

Junk: slang for a narcotic drug, usually referring to heroin.

Viet Cong: a communist army in Vietnam who fought against the American troops (and therefore the Australians who were supporting the Americans) during the Vietnam War.

Q Why do you think the patients respond so well to Nick's rather detached style of direction when he first arrives?

Q Henry explains his personal connection to the opera in this scene by relating elements of it to his own life. Choose another character and identify how he or she has made a connection with the story in *Così Fan Tutte*.

Act Two, Scene One (pp.57–68)

Summary: *The characters rehearse with music for the first time; Cherry introduces the fake shock treatment to the opera; there is a discussion about love and what it means to different characters; Zac contributes his interpretation of* Così Fan Tutte *with his set design and poster; Roy explains his dream of what the opera represents; there's a blackout in the theatre during which several things happen – Zac gropes Ruth and she slaps him, Cherry tries to kiss Lewis, Julie and Lewis do kiss and when the lights come back on the others see Julie and Lewis' kiss.*

Roy's performance with the shock treatment equipment is a good example of the use of black comedy in this text. Roy's pretence is at first amusing because Cherry is so matter of fact about it, and because it is so at odds with the love story of the opera. But quickly it becomes disturbing, as Roy's performance is so convincing that first Lewis and then the audience start to wonder if he is actually receiving the shocks (either by accident or because Cherry has intentionally deceived him). This experience is confronting, being such a serious issue, but it suddenly swings back into comedy as Roy ends his performance and says 'had you all going there, didn't I?' with the word 'all' encompassing not just Lewis and the other patients but the audience as well (p.60). This is an example of how black comedy uses humour to present sensitive issues: the scene not only makes us laugh, but makes us think about the use of shock treatment and about the underlying concerns about treatments for depression.

It is in this scene that the characters discuss what love means to each of them. The theme of 'love', and the notion of fidelity or faithfulness, is constantly present in the text, as it is a central motif of the opera, but this is the first time the characters openly discuss love. As well as giving us a little more insight into the characters' lives, backgrounds and emotional states, the scene helps us see the variety of ways in which they relate to the opera. For Julie, love, like drugs, is about 'being on the edge' (p.61) and perhaps this is why she's enjoying being involved in the opera. For Roy, 'music is what love between humans should be' (p.61), which is an idealistic and symbolic view of love. Henry, once again, makes links between the opera and his own life, and in the process reveals that he was once married (p.64).

Key point

Zac, when discussing his set design, claims 'I can't stand real things. If I could put up with reality I wouldn't be in here' (p.62). In a way, this speaks for all the patients and explains what 'madness' means to them: an inability to face the 'real' world in a 'normal' way. Each of the patients' behavioural problems is a way of avoiding reality.

Just when some of the patients are making progress in the rehearsals (Ruth, for example, is finally grasping the concept of 'pretending' and distinguishing between a theatrical 'reality' and a *real* reality), the theatre is plunged into darkness, recalling all the symbolic associations of darkness from the opening of the play. Even though Lewis was gaining confidence and starting to really have an idea of what he was doing with the opera, the darkness reminds us that the whole situation is still challenging and uncertain. Similarly, it reminds us that stability is not to be taken for granted. The patients in the institution are always maintaining a fragile balance between functional lives and damaged lives, and this is equally true for Lewis and for the audience – we are all, symbolically, submerged into an unexpected darkness.

The blackout allows the patients to let go of their habitual defences: in feeling physically vulnerable in the dark, they seem willing to become more emotionally vulnerable too. Ruth becomes braver, telling a very personal story and then standing up for herself, both verbally and physically, when Zac tries to grope her. Cherry's affection for Lewis reaches a climax, as she searches desperately for him, hoping, as usual, to feed him a sandwich, and to be close to him in the darkness. She doesn't realise that Julie and Lewis are already very close to each other and they kiss just as the lights come back on. All of these events happen quickly, in the confusion of the darkness (or semi-darkness, depending on how a director interprets the scene – the stage directions assume that the audience can dimly see what is going on), and in the chaos the emotional climax parallels that of the final scene in the first act. This ensures that the energy of the play is maintained after the interruption of interval.

The scene ends with Cherry's angry threat towards Julie: another example of black comedy, as we are encouraged to laugh in the face of the normally serious issue of physical violence. Once again, the play is not endorsing or making light of physical violence, nor even Cherry's uncontrollable emotional state. Rather it presents a normally sensitive issue in the context of comedy, inviting us to think more deeply about the issue itself.

Key vocabulary

Charlatan: someone who makes pretence at knowledge they do not have, especially in the medical or healing professions; an impostor.

Mesmer: Franz Mesmer, a controversial 18th-century physician who developed a theory about the magnetic fluids in the human body and proposed corresponding cures using magnets and early forms of hypnotism.

Q What does Ruth mean by 'the more real it is, the more real it is' (p.60) and 'comedy is better when it's real' (p.61)? How can this help explain how black comedy works?

Q Roy is disappointed with the progress of the opera – he says 'it's not like the real thing' (p.63). What does 'reality' mean to Roy, and how does this relate to his speech about his vision and his dream for the opera (several lines later)?

Act Two, Scene Two (pp.68–72)

Summary: *Lucy visits the theatre and she and Lewis have an ideological and personal conflict; Doug reappears and provokes them into further conflict.*

This scene provides a contrast to the previous one, both in terms of length and content. It is much briefer, and is essentially an argument between Lewis and Lucy.

Key point

Lucy asks Lewis to choose between 'going to the moratorium meeting or staying here' (in the theatre); she pushes him to 'make a choice!' (p.69). Lewis chooses: 'Mozart. I'm not going to let them down' (p.70). This is the point where he most clearly articulates his choice, not just for this moment but also in the long term. He chooses the patients, and he chooses the opera, with all that it represents (love and a respect for idealism), over Lucy and Nick and his previous priorities in life.

Lewis and Lucy's discussion echoes some of the themes that were prominent in Act Two, Scene One: most notably love and fidelity. Lewis and Lucy argue about love and fidelity in both abstract and concrete terms. Lucy accuses Lewis of being preoccupied with love, which she believes is 'an emotional indulgence for the privileged few' (p.70). She argues that there are social and political issues that are far more important than love, with the implication that the opera, and Lewis' choice of work, is an indulgent waste of time. Their conflict over the value of love and fidelity quickly becomes more concrete when Lewis accuses Lucy of having an affair with Nick and she confirms it. Lewis is comparing this to the narrative of the opera (much as Henry and others have done in previous scenes), which infuriates Lucy, when suddenly Doug arrives and feeds the conflict, telling Lucy that Lewis has been 'shagging Julie' (p.72).

It is ironic that Lucy is refuting the value of idealistic notions like love and fidelity, and yet love and fidelity are exactly what she and Lewis are arguing about. Lucy fails to acknowledge that these are real concerns, which make an impact on people's lives, even if they are not as 'important' as politics and the state of the world.

Key point

Doug's behaviour in this scene echoes his compulsive fire-starting activities. Previously, he has lit actual fires, delighting in the destructive and exhilarating power of flame. Here, he is delighting in the destructive powers of feeding a symbolic fire: he clearly enjoys provoking both Lewis and Lucy and watching their relationship 'combust' in response.

Q What does 'love' mean for Lewis, and what does it mean for Lucy?

Q How does Lewis and Lucy's argument about love in this scene reflect the discussion between Lewis and Julie (pp.32–3)?

Act Two, Scene Three (pp.73–80)

Summary: *Everyone prepares for the performance; Lewis talks Roy out of his stage fright; Lewis hits Nick and Henry stands up for Lewis; Ruth stands up to Zac; Julie and Lewis share a last quick kiss; Zac overdoses on his medication.*

Lewis' decision to choose the opera over his life with Lucy and Nick has strengthened him, and in this scene we see him managing to keep the patients relatively calm as the stress of the imminent performance takes its toll on all of them. When Nick arrives to wish him luck, Lewis argues with him about the relationship with Lucy and, yet again, we see that love and fidelity are important in people's lives, even though Nick, like Lucy, argues that these frivolous concepts are less meaningful than the social politics for which he fights. When Nick insults the patients as he did in Act One, Scene Four, again calling them loonies, Lewis can no longer stand it and he hits Nick. In physically rejecting Nick and their friendship, with the shared past it represents, Lewis gains the support of Henry, and it is clear where Lewis' loyalties lie. The last moments of the scene build into a nervous frenzy as the patients prepare for their performance. Nowra uses this moment to create a strong image of the parallels between the theatre and 'madness'.

Q How do Lewis' interactions with the patients differ here, compared to the earlier scenes?

Act Two, Scene Four (pp.80–4)

Summary: *The opera is finally performed and we see the final scene; there's a panic when they realise Zac hasn't recovered yet and there is no music; the cast pull together to cover up this moment, improvising until Lewis starts the music.*

This short scene is the culmination of all the preparations. The *Così* audience now become the *Così Fan Tutte* audience as the opera's final scene is performed. As before, the patients face obstacles that threaten the success of the opera (this time, the temporary loss of music) and, just as they have all along, they overcome the challenges. At last, the end of the performance is reached at the conclusion of this scene.

Key point

The performance of the opera uses the common play-within-a-play theatrical technique. Examples can be found in Shakespeare's plays – such as *Hamlet* and *A Midsummer Night's Dream* – and many other plays. In this case it is another way of questioning what is 'real' by adding yet another layer of 'illusion'.

Q How do the lines from *Così Fan Tutte* in this scene comment on the action in *Così* itself?

Act Two, Scene Five (pp.84–9)

Summary: *Lewis accepts Justin's congratulations and learns that Roy has been complaining about his direction all along; he farewells each of the patients; Lewis delivers a monologue to the audience about what became of each of the patients, and then turns out the lights and leaves.*

This scene neatly concludes the script, allowing Lewis to say goodbye individually to each character (except Zac, who is presumably still comatose somewhere). Some of the farewells are quite amusing, like Roy's list of criticisms for Lewis (p.88) and Cherry's sneaky 'tonguey' kiss (p.86). Others are quite poignant, like Ruth's final line, 'I hate goodbyes, so when the others come out tell them I'm waiting outside counting the stars' (p.85). Others are somewhere in between, like Henry's surprise revelation that his paralysed arm is not a physical condition, since the symptom has suddenly moved to his right arm. He explains it very simply: 'it changes' (p.86). The combination of these goodbyes provides us with the mixture of pathos and humour which has become familiar throughout the course of this black comedy.

The final moment of the play echoes the very first moment, and also the blackout in the middle of the text. Lewis announces that it is 'time to turn out the lights', and then he does (p.89). He returns the stage to the state it was in for the opening moment – empty and dark.

Q How is the darkness here different from the darkness during the blackout, or the darkness at the beginning of the opening scene? What does this last darkness represent?

Q Has Lewis changed through his experience with *Così Fan Tutte*? If so, how?

Q Have the other characters changed through their experience with *Così Fan Tutte*? If so, how?

CHARACTERS & RELATIONSHIPS

Lewis Riley

Key quotes

'[*hesitantly*] This is an unusual position for me ... I directed some plays at university ... and, well ... this is my first year out –' (p.7)

'In a way you're sort of testing yourself by coming here?' (Julie to Lewis, p.32)

'I'm not going to let them down.' (p.70)

'Without love the world wouldn't mean much.' (p.70)

Lewis is a version of Louis Nowra, but it is important not to confuse the two. Even if Lewis is grounded in reality, he is still a fictional character.

Passivity

Lewis is the central character in *Così*, although for a long time he is very passive and therefore other characters sometimes overshadow him. Lewis is unsure about what exactly he is supposed to be doing in the asylum, and this seems to represent how he feels about his life generally. Rather than making decisions, he tends to try to please other people by agreeing to whatever they want him to do. Even his political beliefs appear to simply be based on those of Lucy and Nick. Similarly, later, when he makes his statement about love being important in the world, he seems to have borrowed the line from somewhere – maybe from one of the patients or even from *Così Fan Tutte* – since his actions don't really seem to reflect this belief. He doesn't pursue his relationship with Lucy, and seems only briefly disappointed that a relationship with Julie is out of the question (p.87).

Lewis' indecisiveness and lack of confidence are present in his very first line, 'don't know' (p.1). Not long after this, Justin mistakes him for a patient in the asylum. This indicates how uncertain and hesitant Lewis' identity is: not only is he not sure of himself, but he does not communicate a confident persona to anyone else. In the first few pages, the stage directions refer to Lewis' *'apprehension'* (p.4), and instruct the actor to deliver his lines *'uncomfortably'* (p.4), *'uncertainly'* (p.5) and *'hesitantly'* (p.7). This is partly because Lewis is new in the situation, but it also gives us a good indication of his confidence levels (low) and his capacity to act decisively and strongly (poor!).

Compassion

Lewis tries hard to be sensitive to the patients, never to judge them and not to destroy their dreams when he can help it. He genuinely wants this situation to work out for the best, even if he is not entirely confident about what the situation *is*, or even what 'the best' might be. He regularly tries to mediate the often volatile situations involving the patients, and to support them as much as possible. Early examples are when he tries to address Ruth's concerns about the cappuccinos, even when those concerns are contradictory and irrational (p.10); when he tries to cheer Roy up by showing an interest in the opera, even though the production sounds impossible (p.12); and when he decides to support the lie to Justin about who started the fire in the toilets (p.22).

Strength

For a while Lewis struggles through rehearsals, unsure of what he is doing, unsure how to keep all the patients happy at the same time. He is unable to stop Doug from lighting fires, Roy from creatively hijacking the whole project, or even Cherry from trying to force-feed him. The turning point is when Nick visits and upsets Henry. Lewis makes an active decision to support Henry and the rest of the patients instead of his rather insensitive friend Nick (pp.49–50). When Henry threatens to leave, Lewis physically stands up to him, finally showing strength and leadership. This has a positive result when Henry agrees to stay, and even admits his fondness for Lewis. From this moment his dedication to the opera is clear, even when things get difficult. He later articulates this commitment to Lucy when, in the second act, she asks him to choose between the moratorium meeting and the opera rehearsal, effectively asking him to choose between her and them (pp.69–70). Lewis chooses Mozart, the patients and love, over the war protest, Lucy and politics.

Key point

Although Lewis and Roy are in almost constant conflict, together they are the team who see the opera through to its performance, motivating and supporting the patients in their own way.

Q Do you think that Lewis has really grown and changed by the end of the play – how do you think he might behave now at the beginning of another new and challenging project?

Roy

Key quotes

'He loves the theatre apparently. A great enthusiast when he gets going. He has his down periods like a lot of people, but he's your support, your natural energiser.' (Justin to Lewis, about Roy, p.3)

'Without this opera having been composed, there would be just a clanging, banging, a bedlam all around us.' (p.13)

'I aim for the stars, Jerry, is that such a bad thing –' (p.15)

'I had a dream, Jerry … a world that was as far removed from this depressing asylum as possible.' (p.63)

Roy is the driving force behind the institution's production of *Così Fan Tutte*. The opera is his idea, his dream and his vision; his passion for it regularly pushes Lewis through seemingly insurmountable difficulties. Roy cares about the opera more than anything else, including the feelings of others. He is dismissive of people's concerns about being able to do the opera, and often snaps at the other patients when their behaviour doesn't fit in with his vision. He is impatient, passionate, and stubborn.

Mood swings

Roy's behaviour seems to characterise bipolar disorder (once known as manic depression), with his moods fluctuating between manic (excitable, erratic, impulsive) and depressed. However, as with the other patients, he is never labelled in the text as suffering from a particular disorder. This encourages us to see Roy more holistically, not to judge him on his disorder but to see him as a character who happens to suffer from severe mood swings, and whose exuberance is sometimes a useful thing and sometimes a problem.

The music of the spheres

Roy first explains what the opera really means to him at the end of the first scene. He describes how the beauty of the music is able to make sense of the world for him, and how it represents 'the harmony of the spheres', and he is confident that he can make the rest of the group understand this magic (p.13). This image of a celestial and magical harmony is repeated regularly, as he refers over and over to 'the music of the spheres' (p.30, p.35, p.63).

For Roy, this beautiful vision of the opera represents a childhood he wishes he had experienced. He describes this childhood to Lewis as one filled with high culture, elegance, music, joy and a lovely mother (pp.63–4). It isn't until later that Cherry tells Lewis (and therefore the audience) that Roy actually grew up 'in orphanages and being farmed out to foster parents' (p.76). Roy's imagined childhood, then, like his vision of the opera, is a way for him to escape the mundane and depressing real world, and create something more bearable and more beautiful in his mind.

Jerry Lewis and Dean Martin

On meeting Lewis, Roy nicknames him 'Jerry', exclaiming 'we'll be like Jerry Lewis and Dean Martin' (p.3). While the nickname seems affectionate, and indeed Roy is initially complimentary and flattering, he gradually spends more and more time criticising 'Jerry'. He takes out his frustrations on Lewis, blaming him whenever the rehearsals don't live up to his dream. When Ruth struggles to grasp the concept of pretending, Roy tells Doug that Lewis 'couldn't direct a poofter to a man's dunny' (p.10). After Doug sets fire to the toilets, Roy says 'we'll get a new director then. Thank God!' (p.22). When Henry refuses to speak in the first rehearsal, Roy blames Lewis' directing abilities: 'couldn't direct traffic down a one way street' (p.28). And after Doug is sent back to the closed ward, yet again Roy takes it out on Lewis, muttering: 'couldn't direct a nymphomaniac to a stag night' (p.36). Despite all this criticism, Roy is often quick to praise Lewis, too, when he feels positive. For example, he praises Lewis for staying inside at lunch to look over the translation: 'you're like the best directors, a glutton for work' (p.16).

Roy's ambivalence (two contradictory feelings about one person or thing) towards Lewis is typical of his quick shifts in mood, and shows that Roy's reactions aren't always based directly on what is actually occurring around him, but perhaps on some other 'reality' that exists in his mind. This also applies to Roy's lively praise of Nick's directing abilities. Nick really has done nothing to deserve Roy's praise, but Roy is instantly enthusiastic, and says to Lewis 'he's brilliant, isn't he?' (p.43), and, moments later, 'brilliant! Everything is coming alive. Everything matches my vision' (p.45). Roy is so desperate to sustain his illusion of beauty and harmony that he latches on to any glimpse of success in the rehearsal room.

Q How deeply do you think Roy believes in his own fantasies – does he really believe the story he tells about his childhood, or is he aware that he is creating a fiction?

Doug

Key quotes

'What have I done now?' (p.7)

'Let's do a rock musical. A nude, tribal, let's make love not war, man, rock opera.' (p.15)

'Don't blame me, blame my mother.' (p.23)

'This theatre would have burnt like a real beauty. [*A beat.*] My motto is to try and try again.' (p.85)

Doug is the most dangerous of the residents in the opera cast. He has a history of pyromania (but, as with the other characters, is never labelled in the text). He continues to try to set things on fire, first the toilets (pp.21–2) and then the theatre itself (p.34). He unnerves the meeker characters, like Ruth, but finds an equal sparring partner in Cherry, with whom he regularly exchanges insults. While he is crass, meddlesome and often rude and offensive, he tends not to bear much malice towards anyone. Even his slanging matches with Cherry are fairly affectionate. He likes to act tough, but when he escapes from the closed ward and comes back to the theatre, he is only joking when he says that he's come to kill Lewis for taking his role (p.71). Instead, he seems to have come to check what's been happening with the opera in his absence, and he does choose to come to the opera performance at the end.

Key point

Doug is one of the characters who is changed the least by his involvement in the opera. His behaviour is consistent throughout, and he seems to take everything in his (admittedly rather unstable) stride. As Lewis notes in his closing monologue, Doug, predictably, is suspected of burning down the theatre shortly after the opera took place.

Q How is Doug's pyromania a form of escapism and a way of dealing with reality, as is the behaviour of the other patients?

Henry

Key quotes

'Bit shy, the old Henry. Part of this project is to bring out people like Henry.' (Justin, p.4)

'Look, Henry, you're a failure, as a human being and as a lawyer. *Così* offers you a chance to do something successful at least once in your dismal life.' (Roy, p.27)

Henry, an ex-lawyer, seems to suffer from some form of social phobia, which may be linked with his severe stutter. Henry barely speaks for the first half of the text, and has only four lines up until the end of the first act, when he breaks his silence in an angry and passionate outburst provoked by Nick's communist leanings. It is at this point that Henry finally overcomes his debilitating fear of, or at least reluctance towards, speaking. Once he begins, he is fuelled by his own anger and can hardly stop, and even his stutter partly disappears.

Henry's anger at Nick, and then at Lewis, springs from his respect for his own father, who fought in the Korean War. Henry feels that Nick and Lewis' support of the Viet Cong (America's, and therefore Australia's enemy) is traitorous behaviour, and shows a lack of respect for men like his father who went to war to protect Australia. Tied up with this anger is Henry's resentment of the way *Così Fan Tutte* portrays women. Again his reaction is very personal – he feels that the depiction of women as unfaithful is offensive to the memory of his mother, and the many women like her, who remained faithful to their soldier-partners.

Henry's anger gives him the physical strength to attack Nick in defence of his parents' honour (pp.46–7), and then the emotional strength to admit that he does not want to hit Lewis, but in fact actually likes him (p.49). After this climax for Henry in Act One, Scene Four, he rarely feels the need to speak again for the rest of the play, although when he does, he is clearly more at ease – for example, when he volunteers the personal information about his marriage (pp.64–5). Similarly, he feels comfortable rehearsing the opera, and even sings along to the recorded music when Lewis says nobody needs to: 'I ffffelt like it' (p.57).

Although Henry dies soon after the opera, it is clear that he is one of the characters who benefited most from the experience; the opera actually did succeed in bringing Henry out, as Justin hoped it might.

Q Why do you think Nowra chooses to write Henry's death into Lewis' closing monologue? What else do you think Henry might have gone on to do after the opera, and how would this have changed the message his character conveys?

Julie

Key quotes

'I like doing theatre, even though it's my first time ... I like it because I'm doing something ... Getting out of my ward. God, how I hate that ward.' (p.36)

'... not to be on drugs, whatever sort, is like being in limbo for me. Drugs make me feel sort of living.' (p.37)

'I need something stable in my life. I need my girlfriend.' (p.87)

Julie's parents had her committed to the asylum because of her substance abuse, but she resents being there and feels that the staff 'don't know how to deal with drug users' (p.32). For Julie, the opera makes her time in the asylum bearable. This is not just because she is interested in the opera itself, but also because she is clearly attracted to Lewis from the beginning, and Lewis returns the interest.

Julie and Lewis' relationship reaches its peak during the blackout in Act Two, when they kiss (p.68). They also share a quick kiss 'for good luck' before the performance (p.80), but it is the first kiss that is more significant: the stage directions describe it as *'passionate'*. It is interrupted by the lights coming back on (p.68) and seen by the rest of the patients, which infuriates Cherry but seems not to bother anyone else.

Julie is articulate and enjoys talking to Lewis, and they have several discussions about love and fidelity. Although Doug, Roy and Cherry make regular reference to the obvious attraction between them, Julie and Lewis do not discuss the possibility of a relationship until after the opera, when they are saying their goodbyes. It is at this point that Julie reveals that she has a girlfriend outside the asylum, and that she intends to go back to her.

Q Lewis argues that he is not cheating on Lucy, and that she is cheating on him (p.72). Do you think Lewis and Julie's relationship qualifies as infidelity (in that they both have partners outside the institution)?

Cherry

Key quotes

'This is the best part, isn't it? Not having to eat lunch in a ward. But in a theatre!' (p.20)

'With someone like you I could be true and faithful.' (to Lewis, p.34)

'Kiss him again and I'll break your fuckin' arm.' (to Julie, p.68)

Cherry, hot-headed and overly amorous, is preoccupied with food, and is emotionally volatile, making constant threats of violence, mostly against Doug or Julie. She develops a quick and firm affection for Lewis and does not recognise that her infatuation is unrequited. She is jealous of Lewis' developing relationship with Julie, and spends every spare minute trying to feed Lewis sandwiches and to be close to him.

Q How do you think Cherry has ended up in the institution?

Zac

Key quotes

'I'm prepared to play the pissy score for the whole opera, only if I do the overture my way, or else it's exit the pianist.' (p.30)

'I can't stand real things. If I could put up with reality I wouldn't be in here.' (p.62)

Zac, a musician, arrives into the narrative late (too late to be introduced by Justin) and leaves early (too soon for Lewis to farewell him), and in between, he is often barely present. He is usually heavily drugged, and rarely participates in discussions, with the exception of the scene in which he presents his set design and his poster.

Ruth

Key quotes

'I'm not going to sing a song that is not word perfect. You don't want me to make a fool of myself, do you?' (p.13)

'I can live with illusion as long as I know it's illusion …' (p.26)

'Comedy is better when it's real.' (p.61)

Ruth's behaviour characterises a form of obsessive-compulsive disorder, an anxiety disorder. She routinely seeks reassurance and needs detailed routines to feel comfortable. She is also preoccupied with truth (perhaps her name is a loose pun!), reality, and illusion, and her journey in the play is one of coming to terms with the different kinds of 'truths' around her.

Ruth, like Henry, is one of the few characters who manages to benefit from her involvement in the opera. The turning point for Ruth is when she defends herself against criticism from Cherry, making a distinction between herself and her character. This amuses Lewis, and he enjoys teasing Ruth with the fact that she has, finally, begun to 'pretend' onstage. Although Ruth is reluctant to admit this, she has clearly made progress in reaching a point where she is *able* to admit it.

Ruth is described in Lewis' closing monologue as having successfully left the asylum; she is one of few characters to achieve this.

Lucy

Key quotes

'She's into politics. She hates talk about love. She thinks it's icky ... She hates me doing an opera about love and fidelity while thousands of Vietnamese are being killed by American troops.' (Lewis, p.33)

'I have sex with him and sleep with you.' (to Lewis, p.71)

'Lucy and Nick? Well they didn't last long as both were not into fidelity.' (Lewis, p.89)

Lucy is Lewis' girlfriend, although it is never very clear why: the play does not show us any affection or chemistry between the two of them. Lewis himself seems uncommitted to the relationship: when Doug asks if he plans to marry Lucy, Lewis says 'who knows?' (p.18), and when he kisses Julie (p.68, p.80) his behaviour supports this lack of commitment. Lucy doesn't show much faith in their relationship either. The bond between them has lost its spark (if there ever was one) and the couple's lives are drifting apart. It is no surprise to learn that Lucy is having an affair with Nick. When Lewis asks if she and Nick are having an affair, Lucy says bluntly: 'of course' (p.70).

Although Lucy's infidelity with Nick is not revealed until almost the end of the play (p.70), it is hinted at from the very beginning. Not only do Lucy and Nick leave the theatre together, abandoning Lewis (p.2), but it is also clear, even in this first scene, that Lucy and Nick are on a wavelength that does not include Lewis. Lucy and Nick share priorities – both are passionate about their active student politics – and they both lack interest in, or respect for, what Lewis is doing. Lucy's passion for politics mirrors Roy's passion for the opera.

Lucy only appears in two of the play's nine scenes, while Lewis is in every scene; this contributes to the impression that she and Lewis are drifting out of each other's lives.

Q In what ways is Lucy different from Roy? Which of these two characters influences Lewis more?

Nick

Key quotes

'Mad actors are bad enough, but madmen ...' (p.1)

'My friend, Nick, is the one who knows all about theatre, only he's more interested in politics.' (Lewis, p.32)

'Women shouldn't come between mates ... It's only sex.' (p.77)

Nick is a close friend of Lewis, and lives with him and Lucy. But it is clear that Nick, like Lucy, no longer shares much with Lewis. Their priorities and beliefs no longer seem compatible and, in two out of the three scenes in which Nick appears, he and Lewis fight: first verbally (in Act One) and then physically (in Act Two).

Nick, believes, as does Lucy, that there are social and political issues much more important and valid than love and fidelity, and he thinks Lewis is wasting his time in the asylum. He doesn't appreciate the meaning that the opera has for the patients, and sees both the patients' attitudes and the opera itself as 'right wing crap' (p.47). Nick has a low tolerance for the quirks of the patients, and is insensitive towards them, making a joke about their situation and singing a politically incorrect song about a 'funny farm' (p.41, p.77). (This is an actual song, a popular novelty song from the mid 1960s by an artist called Jerry Samuels. It was controversial at the time.)

Q What do Lewis and Nick have in common?

THEMES, IDEAS & VALUES

Love and fidelity

Key quotes

'Love is not so important nowadays.' ... 'What planet are you from?' (Lewis and Roy, p.10)

'You believe in free love and that sort of thing?' ... 'Free love is a hard concept to define.' (Doug and Lewis, p.18)

'"Love is the last gasp of bourgeois romanticism" she says.' (Lewis about Lucy, p.33)

'I've always thought that love was being foolish and stupid ... Love is hallucinating without drugs.' (Julie, p.61)

'Love is what you feel when you don't have enough emotion left to hate.' (Roy, p.61)

'Without love the world wouldn't mean much.' (Lewis, p.70)

Love is not just the central theme of the opera but also the central theme of *Così*. The particular aspect of love that is the focus of both musical and play is fidelity: the notion of faithfulness, commitment and loyalty.

The play explores many aspects of the theme of love and fidelity, and the characters present slightly different perspectives, by giving us opinions on what love is; whether fidelity is important or even possible; and what love actually means to them. Some of the characters are firm about their positions from start to finish, and others change their mind or develop differing perspectives along the way. Not only each character, but also each scene can offer a new interpretation of this theme. In this way, Nowra's play considers the ideas of love and fidelity, without necessarily offering definitive opinions. Instead, *Così* presents a variety of social values and perspectives associated with love and fidelity, some of which are discussed below.

Love is an indulgence

Lucy and Nick are the characters who most strongly endorse this idea. They both believe that other social and political issues are much more important than love. Lucy's speech to Lewis in Act Two, Scene Two explains her justification for this: 'after bread, a shelter, equality, health, procreation, money comes maybe love. Do you think the starving masses give a fuck about love?' (p.70). Nick, too, espouses this view: 'only mad people in this day and age would do a work about love and infidelity' (p.41). On the night of the performance of *Così Fan Tutte*, Nick explains to Lewis why he and Lucy would prefer to be out celebrating the moratorium than supporting their friend at his production. Nick says, 'you don't understand, Lewis – today Australia was changed forever. She doesn't want to see an opera about a few upper class twits' (p.76).

In Nick and Lucy's belief system, fighting for their political ideals involves struggling to improve the quality of life for socially disadvantaged or politically oppressed peoples. This is their primary motivation, and it certainly means more to them than anything as frivolous as love. Although they are having a relationship, it seems to have more to do with shared politics and sex than it does with love. When she admits her affair to Lewis, Lucy says 'It's only a fling. It doesn't mean anything ... I have sex with him and sleep with you' (p.71), implying that sex is somehow separate from love, and that faithfulness doesn't really matter – particularly when it comes to physical sex. Nick, too, says 'it's only sex' when he talks about the affair, implying that faithfulness is not important to him either (p.77). Lewis confirms this in his closing monologue when he says that neither Nick nor Lucy cared about fidelity (p.89). The implication, based on what we have already seen of their characters, is that social welfare and basic human rights are the values Nick and Lucy support, rather than individual emotional fulfilment.

Key point

Although the play, through Lucy and Nick, strongly presents an argument for the fact that love should be secondary to basic human needs, at the same time it supports the notion that love is a universal experience to which we can all relate: otherwise, why write a play which is underpinned by a debate about the importance of love?

Lewis, at the beginning of the play, shares Nick and Lucy's political beliefs. When Roy first introduces the idea of doing *Così Fan Tutte*, Lewis objects on the grounds that an opera about fidelity is not really relevant in a society and an era where war is impacting on millions of lives (p.10). Lewis' objection represents the idea that love is an indulgence available only to those who enjoy the privilege of a stable social existence. This idea, in turn, endorses the value of universal human rights.

As the play progresses, however, Lewis begins to shift his perspective to include the importance of love. This is not to say that the value of human rights is ever contested in the play, but rather that Lewis comes to see love as something that is always important, not just something which can only have meaning when every other practical aspect of life is fulfilled (as Lucy suggests). Instead, through his experiences with the patients and how they relate to the themes of the opera, Lewis gradually conceives of love as something that underlies all else: 'without love the world wouldn't mean much' (p.70).

Free love

The concept of 'free love' is one that *Così* explores in passing. Free love is a philosophy of individuals' rights to freedom in how they choose to engage in romantic relationships, as opposed to relationships that are regulated by convention or imposed by society. The term has also become something of a cliché in the context of the social revolution of the 1970s, and in *Così* Doug seems to hold a fairly simplistic view of free love as meaning no more than the freedom to be promiscuous and unfaithful.

By making Doug the character most preoccupied with it, Nowra portrays the notion of free love in a fairly negative way: Doug is the most dangerous of the patients, and also one of those who provides the most comedy (through his blunt lines and his lack of inhibitions). Doug also generally refers to free love in a way that is potentially offensive, because he is challenging Lewis' relationship with Lucy and Lewis' belief that Lucy is faithful. He even spreads it around the asylum that Lewis and Lucy are into free love, when, as Lewis puts it, the fact is that Lucy is 'not into marriage' (p.33), which is not exactly the same thing.

Nick is the other character to bring up the issue of free love – his behaviour (in having the affair with Lucy, and also in the way that he talks about the affair) echoes what Doug means when he talks about 'free love'. Even when Nick speaks of the opera, he describes it as a story about 'love and infidelity' (p.41) rather than love and *fidelity*, which is how others see it. Fidelity just doesn't mean anything to Nick, and he is much more likely to believe in free love, although he never really addresses it in the text except to say to Lewis, 'Lucy's not possessive about you, I'm not possessive about her. What's the fuss?' (p.76). Nick is a character who is not terribly likeable to an audience; his lack of sensitivity towards the patients and his lack of real support for Lewis make us less inclined to feel empathy for him. In aligning Doug and Nick with the idea of free love, the play encourages us not to endorse free love, as we are encouraged not to sanction other aspects of these characters' behaviour.

Q Although Lewis is the central character, and one with whom we are encouraged to empathise, he is unfaithful to Lucy when he kisses Julie. How do we account for this behaviour, which is exactly what we are invited to condemn when it involves Nick and Lucy?

Love is like …

Each character has their own way of viewing love, and *Così Fan Tutte* gives them a reason to discuss love. The things that they say about love give us some insight into their prior experiences with love, and also into their experiences of life in general. For example, when Lewis says 'without love the world wouldn't mean much' (p.70), he indicates that although his current relationship with Lucy is failing, and although his attraction to Julie can never really be pursued, he still believes love is a vital aspect of human life. This statement of his is fairly broad, and not really supported by detail, but it shows that he believes deeply and firmly in love. Here are some examples of other characters' statements about love:

- Cherry, about *Così Fan Tutte*: it 'is just another thing about the battle of the sexes' (p.11), and 'most women fight hard to keep men out of their pants' (p.61).
- Nick, about the women's characters in Così Fan Tutte: 'you want to remain true to your lovers. It's an old fashioned concept …' (p.43).
- Henry: 'whether women can remain true is a ttttragedy' (p.49).
- Julie, about love: 'it's about being on the edge and I like being on the edge' (p.61).
- Roy: 'love is what you feel when you don't have enough emotion left to hate … hate is a much more pure emotion … you have enemies for life, but never lovers' (p.61).

Q What does each statement above tell us about the characters and their experiences of love? For example, Cherry's lines suggest that her experiences of love have been fraught with conflict. Her unrequited love for Lewis might be a way of experiencing love with*out* conflict, as there is no real relationship.

Madness and mental health

Key quotes

'... a madman is someone who arrives at a fancy dress party dressed in the Emperor's new clothes.' (p.7)

'Do you think they'll get the idea that the toy soldiers symbolise real soldiers? ... You're dealing with a mad audience, you know.' (p.57)

'It's not divine madness like some people think, there's no such thing as divine madness, madness is just madness.' (p.61)

Così proposes the idea that 'madness' is not always a simple psychological or psychiatric diagnosis, but is sometimes a matter of perspective or judgement. Justin's comment about the Emperor's new clothes could be just a euphemism for naked (the reference comes from a Hans Christian Andersen fairytale about an Emperor who is tricked into believing he is wearing an invisible cloak, when actually he is naked). However, it seems more likely that Justin is describing someone whose behaviour follows a logic of its own but might not appear rational from the outside. In the fairytale, the Emperor believes he is wearing clothes, but everyone else can see he is not. According to Justin's comment, then, 'madness' might be simply behaviour that doesn't necessarily make sense to others, or an interpretation of the world that does not match up with the most common perception.

This definition of madness as subjective is supported by the play's refusal to define the psychological or psychiatric conditions of any of the patients in the institution. Instead, they are presented as people who indulge in extremes of 'normal' behaviour. This illustrates the idea that human behaviour is a spectrum, and that mental stability is not a black-and-white issue. The text endorses a holistic view of human behaviour rather than an attitude of diagnostics and labelling.

Contrastingly, Julie's observation critiques a romantic perception of 'divine madness'. Julie reminds us that madness is not a desirable artistic or philosophical state – it is simply madness. This balances the text's overwhelming support for a non-judgemental view of 'madness'.

Illusion and reality

Key quotes

'I can live with illusion as long as I know it's illusion ...' (p.26)

'It's off-stage, no one will know the difference and they'll think you've got hundreds backstage.' (p.45)

'If I could put up with reality I wouldn't be in here.' (p.62)

The question of what is real and what is an illusion (and whether there is really a difference) underlies *Così*. There are a number of ways the theme of illusion and reality is explored – some very explicit, and others more hidden.

'Did they have instant coffee in Mozart's day?'

Ruth's line above (p.10) characterises her preoccupation with delineating illusion from reality. For Ruth, the process of the opera rehearsals is a process of discovering the concept of 'pretend', and of navigating the uncertain space between what is 'real', what is 'natural' and what is an 'illusion'. Ruth is fixated on tangible details, and she worries about things like having real coffee in the opera, and exactly how many steps to take across the stage. When Lewis tells her simply 'to make it natural' (p.29), Ruth is distressed by the notion, and is desperate to differentiate between 'real' and 'natural' – are they the same thing, or not? She is also concerned with issues that are more philosophical, such as whether 'the audience thinks it's real coffee' (p.26). It is important to her to distinguish between real and pretend, and to keep the two separate. It isn't until Act Two that she begins to enjoy the blurred space between real and pretend, and to appreciate the process of rehearsing and creating a new reality with the opera: 'the more real it is, the more real it is' (p.60).

Theatre as illusion

The theme of reality and illusion is embedded in the play's narrative: the rehearsal and performance of the opera. Theatre is, in a sense, an ultimate illusion, creating characters and lives and inviting an audience to participate in the 'realisation' of this illusion. Not only is *Così* itself a play, but it is also a play about a play (or an opera) – it is a play about the creation of illusion. Together the patients and Lewis engage in the collective building of an illusory world, the world of *Così Fan Tutte*.

The play endorses the view that imagination can be liberating and empowering. As Justin says, the intention of Lewis working with the patients in the theatre is to 'bring them out of their shells' (p.6), and one way to do this is to allow them to create their own reality where normal restrictions do not apply: this new reality is the opera.

While the opera provides an escape for the patients, it is still closely linked to their lives. Each of the characters makes a personal connection with the content of the opera: for example, Henry's comparison of Guglielmo and Ferrando's infidelity with his own father's loyalty (p.48). Cherry, by introducing the shock treatment equipment, brings the patients' own lives into the world of the opera, blending their own realities with the illusion of the theatre.

The play-within-a-play aspect of *Così* is a reminder to the audience that we are watching an illusion, a representation of reality. The questions that the patients confront in rehearsing *Così Fan Tutte* remind us that the performers of *Così* might have faced similar questions: they may have been forced to consider their own beliefs and values about love, for example. This, in turn, reminds us, the audience, to consider our own beliefs and values, comparing them with those of the characters in *Così* and the characters in *Così Fan Tutte*. Nowra emphasises the constructed reality of the theatre in order to encourage his audience to examine their own reality.

Madness as illusion

One of the reasons that rehearsing a performance makes some sense to the patients (even though most of them have never been involved in theatre before) is that they are all familiar with the notion of creating new realities for themselves. The residents of the asylum each have ways of altering their own realities, or constructing new ones that are more bearable – and these strategies tend to reflect the behaviours that have landed the patients in the institution. As Zac notes, 'if I could put up with reality I wouldn't be in here' (p.62), and this is true for most of the patients. The characters each have their own illusion, their own escape from the everyday world. Their collective existence in the institution is another layer of illusion – their 'madness' gives them an escape for as long as they need it.

Reality as illusion

Taken together, these elements in the play suggest that reality itself is a kind of illusion: as Ruth posits, 'an illusion of reality. A real illusion in other words?' (p.26). The value this endorses is that experience is subjective.

The power of music

Key quotes

'There's music, of course.' (p.9)

'This theatre could have been ringing with the music of the spheres, instead of that, a dreadful silence has descended upon us.' (p.35)

'No one cares who wrote the words. Why do you think an opera has music – so no one will have to pay attention to the words!' (p.63)

Music is a central element of *Così*, not least because the play is about the rehearsal of an opera. While we only see one scene from the opera (in Act Two, Scene Four), the notion of music is present throughout the play, and the play as a whole endorses the belief that music has therapeutic powers.

Roy is the patient who most strongly embodies this value, as his longstanding 'dream' of producing *Così Fan Tutte* appears to be one of the few things that gets him through his depressing daily existence in the asylum. The opera is associated with happy childhood memories, whether these are real or imagined: Roy says that his mother played the music for him 'over and over' (p.11). It is not just the theatrical illusion of *Così Fan Tutte* that gives Roy's life meaning, but the music particularly; as he says to Lewis, 'the music of this opera keeps the world in harmony' (p.13). Lewis doesn't think they can do the opera because the music itself is too much of a challenge, but Roy wilfully misinterprets this:

> Straight to the crux of the problem again! I tell you what, we rehearse it like a proper play … then, as we learn the songs, we incorporate them into the stage business we have learnt. (p.16)

For Roy, the music is vital. Later in the play, after the opera has encountered various challenges (such as the loss of Doug), Lewis admits to Roy that they 'just won't have time to learn the music' (p.61), and Roy is completely disheartened: 'music is what love between humans should be. And we've thrown out the music from this opera' (p.61). Music for Roy represents the most idealistic of emotions – love. As Roy reminds us, 'Mozart is about love, not madness' (p.59). A world without music for Roy is a world hardly worth living in. The positive benefits music offers Roy's life are an example of how *Così* presents the idea that music has therapeutic powers.

Other characters, too, help the play endorse this view, most notably Zac, who is comatose much of the time but really comes alive when he can offer a musical contribution. For example, he becomes greatly excited when he brings in his old, battered accordion, and offers to contribute some Wagner to the opera (p.30). While he doesn't find Mozart terribly empowering, for Zac, Wagner has therapeutic power, motivating and exciting him beyond his usual drugged-out state. Wagner's music also eventually gets Zac out of the asylum, as Lewis notes in his closing monologue (p.89). Music, then, for Zac as well as Roy, has the power to motivate and energise.

There are other passing references to the positive benefits of music. For example, Julie asks to borrow Lewis' transistor because she 'wouldn't mind listening to some music' (p.21). When the stress or mundaneness of the asylum become overwhelming, many of the characters turn to music. Ruth can sing and memorises a song for the auditions, and Roy even claims to have heard Henry, who barely speaks, 'humming … he's a natural' (p.12).

Politics and empowerment: the value of theatre

Key quotes

'See, I'm happy coming to this burnt out theatre.' (Julie, p.36)

'He's doing a play that's relevant and he's doing something about the war in Vietnam.' (Lucy, about Nick, p.70)

There is a tension in *Così* between the political and social values of theatre. This is most clearly presented through the differences between Lewis and Nick's priorities. Although Nick is a director too, he gives his political activities priority. The goals he strives towards in his political activities – to make people 'want the war to end … want changes in our society … want to overthrow the establishment' (p.17) – are the same goals he hopes to achieve with his theatre productions. As Lucy notes, what is important about theatre is how to make it 'meaningful and intelligent, like Brecht does' (p.70). Nick refers proudly to his own productions of Brecht's works (p.41) and, as Lewis observes, 'says politics is the real theatre' (p.32). This indicates that he values theatre for its political rather than its artistic significance.

Lewis, on the other hand, once he begins to work with the patients, approaches theatre on the levels of entertainment, illusion, and the value it can bring to the performers' lives. His work is a form of drama therapy: the use of the dramatic arts to help individuals or groups work through problems, increase self-confidence and develop or improve personal and social skills. Lewis also values theatre for its transformative powers, then, but in a more domestic sense than Nick.

Nick and Lucy scorn Lewis for his involvement with the asylum and with *Così Fan Tutte* on the grounds that what he is doing is less important than their large-scale, public efforts to implement social change. But they fail to acknowledge that Lewis is also working towards social change, merely in a smaller, more local context. While Nick and Lucy rehearse Brecht's *Galileo* and engage in protests against the Vietnam War, Lewis is fighting for his own changes through *Così Fan Tutte*: he is trying to bring change to the patients' lives and to give them confidence and the power to take charge of their own realities. Although Lewis is never completely successful (as evidenced by the mixed outcomes he reports for the patients in his closing monologue), the play presents the view that theatre has at least as much value in the context of personal empowerment as it does on a political level.

DIFFERENT INTERPRETATIONS

Different interpretations arise from different responses to a text. These responses can be published in newspapers, journals and books by critics and reviewers, or they can be expressed in discussions among readers in the media, classrooms, book groups and so on. A production of a play is also an interpretation of the text (the script). While there is no single correct reading or interpretation of a text, it is important to understand that an interpretation is more than an 'opinion' – it is the justification of a point of view on the text. To present an interpretation of the text based on your point of view you must use a logical argument and support it with relevant evidence from the text.

Productions and reviews

Così is widely acknowledged as one of Nowra's most successful plays. It remains popular with audiences 17 years after its first production, as evidenced by its extensive republication as a script (the 1994 Currency Press edition has been reprinted at least once every year), and by its regular performances both within and beyond Australia. As Veronica Kelly notes in her book about Nowra and his work, *Così* is 'a favourite with performers, directors and audiences' (Kelly 1998, p.43).

After its first production at Belvoir Street in 1992, reviews of the play were largely positive. Angela Bennie described *Così* as 'hilarious' and 'strong', and discussed the characterisation in detail, especially concentrating on the performances themselves, but referencing their basis in the script. Although Bennie criticised the script for being over length, this was obviously addressed in the later revision (in 1994), when the domestic scenes outside the asylum were removed from the script.

Reviews of more recent productions tend to focus on the theatrical interpretation and therefore to concentrate on performances and directorial choices – response to the text itself is often limited to a positive acknowledgment of Nowra's original script. This allows reviewers to discuss the particular production's interpretation of the script, analysing how the company explores and presents Nowra's themes of love, madness and illusion. Reviews tend to concentrate on the hilarity of the productions, and on how the sensitive issue of mental illness is tackled. International reviews often comment on the use of common Australianisms in the language of the play – an aspect that tends to be ignored in Australian productions as the language habits of the characters are so familiar as to escape notice.

Natalie Bennett's review of a recent production of *Così* in London mentions that a male actor played Ruth as a transvestite. This 'interpretation' of the original script takes extensive liberties, yet seems a valid interpretation. Consider, for example, the extra layer of significance regarding Ruth's obsession with reality and illusion. If she were a male living as a female, this would be one interesting way of exploring her thoughts about what is real and what is not.

Casting

The play is written to accommodate doubling in the cast (one actor playing multiple parts). Specifically, a single actor can play Justin, Nick and Zac, as these characters are never on stage together; and a single character can play Lucy and Julie. The original Company B production cast the show in this way. Often it is more economical for a professional company to cast fewer actors, especially when some roles are very small, like the role of Justin. On the other hand, amateur productions often want to give experience to as many actors as possible, so they may choose to cast one actor for each role.

The doubling of Lucy and Julie is particularly interesting. If a single actor is playing both of these roles, it will encourage an audience to draw very distinct parallels between the characters. Lewis is attracted to both of them, and both women are engaged in unfaithful behaviour (as is Lewis). With these characters played by one actor, there is an implication that perhaps Lewis is attracted to the same things in both of them and/or that they are very similar people. It also raises interesting questions: are we less inclined to judge Lewis' infidelity because on some level (certainly within the illusional reality of the theatre), Lucy and Julie are almost the same person?

The issues raised by this casting are complex, and should not be misread as changing the meaning of the play. However, it is worth considering how this might make an impact on an audience.

Film interpretation

One widely available 'interpretation' of *Così* is the 1996 film version. While Nowra's screenplay does differ in several important ways from his stage play, the film may still be considered an interpretation of the play, as it presents essentially the same narrative, choosing to highlight some aspects and themes over others – just as a stage production might.

In Nowra's preface to the published film script, he describes his negotiations with the film company executives and creative team as he worked on the drafts of the screenplay. Many changes were small details (such as phrasing), but three were particularly significant. The first is the shift of setting, from the 1970s to the 1990s, removing the Vietnam War story and the broader political context. In the film, this is replaced by the more intimate 'politics' of Lewis' own life. The second important change regards Lewis' relationships with Lucy and with Julie. Miramax was reluctant for Lewis and Lucy to split up, preferring that the film have a happy ending, and they were also uncomfortable about Lewis and Julie's kisses. Some changes were made for the American but not the Australian print of the film – for example, in the American version Lewis and Lucy stay together (Kelly 1998, p.54). The final important change is to the ending: the published screenplay concludes with a closing voiceover from Lewis which is more or less the same as in the stage play monologue. However, this was cut from the film, which ends after the opera, thus remaining more optimistic and 'comic'.

The film interpretation, in removing the Vietnam War storyline, shifts the emphasis of *Così* to one of its other themes: love. The differences between Nick and Lewis are no longer about politics, but about how they each perceive the narrative of *Così Fan Tutte*, and about how they each relate to Lucy. This draws the focus more strongly to the idea of infidelity, and even though Lucy doesn't admit to sleeping with Nick in the film version, the issue of love and fidelity is prominent.

The other notable choice in the film interpretation of *Così* is to set many scenes outside the theatre; some in Lewis and Lucy's house, and many in daylight in the 'outside world'. This decision to expand the action beyond the theatre breaks down the boundary between the 'mad' world of the asylum and the 'normal' world of the outside. This is a notion that is already endorsed by the stage play, but the film interpretation makes it even more explicit. This boundary is blurred in many other ways by the film: for example, Doug visits Lewis' house, representing the fact that 'madness' is not simply contained within the theatre but encroaches on the 'normal' world too. Similarly, Lewis spends a night in the asylum when Doug convinces the orderlies that it is Lewis and not he who is the patient.

Two possible interpretations

The following interpretations demonstrate how the same observations can be used to support a positive or a negative evaluation of the text, as long as this judgement is supported with evidence from that text.

Reading 1

In *Così*, Louis Nowra makes fun of mental illness, inappropriately exploiting 'mad' people's suffering for his own comic purposes.

Così is a play which draws its comedy from the portrayal of damaged people who suffer from a variety of conditions, although these conditions are never described or analysed: instead they are generalised and manipulated for comic purposes. For example, Cherry's preoccupation with food (suggesting a dysfunctional relationship with eating) is only ever acknowledged by her attempts to force-feed Lewis, or by Doug's insults about her weight. Similarly, while Ruth appears to suffer from obsessive-compulsive disorder, the implications are never addressed, and her obsession is always grounds for comedy, such as when she struggles with how many steps to take on stage (pp.29–30). There is no evidence in the text of any support for the patients' conditions; instead, they laugh at each other's quirks and unusual behaviours. This encourages the audience to laugh at them too, and to dismiss any concerns they may have about the seriousness of these particular mental illnesses.

Similarly, we are encouraged to laugh at those patients whose behaviour is dangerous to others: particularly Doug. When Justin introduces Doug to Lewis, he makes a light-hearted joke about the fact that Doug should be on medication, but that Lewis should watch out because Doug is 'a bit cheeky the way he won't take it sometimes' (p.5). Justin doesn't equip Lewis with any knowledge, skills or strategies for managing the patients, but instead cheerfully abandons him to negotiate the dangers on his own. The script makes light of Doug's history of pyromania, with the other patients constantly telling him to 'go burn a cat', referring to the incident which resulted in Doug's admission to the asylum.

Finally, the character of Nick represents the script's ultimate insult to mental illness; he jokes about madness, comparing madmen to actors (p.1), and on several occasions he sings the bizarre and provocative song about the funny farm. While Lewis objects to Nick's behaviour, he never justifies his objections with any information that would educate Nick or an audience about how to sensitively approach mental illness.

Taken as a whole, *Così* presents the view that it is acceptable to laugh at mental illness, rather than attempting to explain the conditions or search for more sensitive ways of relating to those who are different.

Reading 2

Louis Nowra's play *Così* is a comedy that sensitively and respectfully portrays the experiences of patients in a mental institution.

Although *Così* is a very funny and entertaining play set in an asylum, we are never encouraged to laugh *at* the patients themselves. Rather, the script endorses a view of 'madness' that suggests human behaviour forms a continuum and that all humans fall somewhere between 'mad' and 'normal'. In this play, much of the behaviour (particularly, but not exclusively, from the patients) leans strongly towards the 'mad' end of the scale, but this is rarely used as evidence that these people are any less human, valuable or functional. Instead, the various behaviours of the patients are portrayed as extreme examples of how any human being might act, and this is where the comedy originates. These characters are not so different from ourselves that we find it impossible to identify with them, but they take things to such extremes that it becomes comical.

While each patient displays traits that remind us of familiar mental illnesses or conditions (such as pyromania, nymphomania, or bipolar disorder), these traits are presented simply as elements of the characters' personalities rather than as symptoms of disorders. For example, Roy's behaviour, which could be described as bipolar disorder, is simply who Roy *is*: he finds himself overwhelmingly excited at some times, but drained and demoralised at other times. When he is excited, his enthusiasm is contagious and he tries to inspire the others to 'aim for the stars!' (p.15); when he is depressed, he says simply 'I'm down' (p.63). We can all recognise these basic human emotions, and in resisting labelling Roy with a particular mental condition, Nowra helps audiences to relate to, rather than judge, the characters.

By breaking down the familiar distinctions between 'mad' and 'normal', Nowra allows us to join Lewis on a journey as he deals with the patients' behaviour, and with his own prejudices and reactions to this behaviour. The comedy, then, becomes an empathetic comedy where we are encouraged to laugh with the characters at the ridiculousness of the situations they find themselves in, rather than at their disabilities or their position in the institution.

Così warmly portrays the challenges faced by this group of patients in the same way that it would illustrate the challenges faced by a group of people outside the asylum. The individual behaviour of patients and the relationships between them contribute to the situation comedy that treats its underlying serious subject matter with respect.

QUESTIONS & ANSWERS

This section focuses on your own analytical writing on the text, and gives you strategies for producing high-quality responses in your coursework and exam essays.

Essay writing – an overview

An essay is a formal and serious piece of writing that presents your point of view on the text, usually in response to a given essay topic. Your 'point of view' in an essay is your interpretation of the meaning of the text's language, structure, characters, situations and events, supported by detailed analysis of textual evidence.

Analyse – don't summarise

In your essays it is important to avoid simply summarising what happens in a text:

- A **summary** is a description or paraphrase (retelling in different words) of the characters and events. For example: 'Macbeth has a horrifying vision of a dagger dripping with blood before he goes to murder King Duncan'.
- An **analysis** is an explanation of the real meaning or significance that lies 'beneath' the text's words (and images, for a film). For example: 'Macbeth's vision of a bloody dagger shows how deeply uneasy he is about the violent act he is contemplating – as well as his sense that supernatural forces are impelling him to act'.

A limited amount of summary is sometimes necessary to let your reader know which part of the text you wish to discuss. However, always keep this to a minimum and follow it immediately with your analysis (explanation) of what this part of the text is really telling us.

Plan your essay

Carefully plan your essay so that you have a clear idea of what you are going to say. The plan ensures that your ideas flow logically, that your argument remains consistent and that you stay on the topic. An essay plan should be a list of **brief dot points** – no more than half a page. It includes:

- your central argument or main contention – a concise statement (usually in a single sentence) of your overall response to the topic. See 'Analysing a sample topic' for guidelines on how to formulate a main contention.
- three or four dot points for each paragraph indicating the main idea and evidence/examples from the text. Note that in your essay you will need to *expand* on these points and *analyse* the evidence.

Structure your essay

An essay is a complete, self-contained piece of writing. It has a clear beginning (the introduction), middle (several body paragraphs) and end (the last paragraph or conclusion). It must also have a central argument that runs throughout, linking each paragraph to form a coherent whole.

See examples of introductions and conclusions in the 'Analysing a sample topic' and 'Sample answer' sections.

The introduction establishes your overall response to the topic. It includes your main contention and outlines the main evidence you will refer to in the course of the essay. Write your introduction *after* you have done a plan and *before* you write the rest of the essay.

The body paragraphs argue your case – they present evidence from the text and explain how this evidence supports your argument. Each body paragraph needs:

- a strong **topic sentence** (usually the first sentence) that states the main point being made in the paragraph
- **evidence** from the text, including some brief quotations
- **analysis** of the textual evidence explaining its significance and **explanation** of how it supports your argument
- **links back to the topic** in one or more statements, usually towards the end of the paragraph.

Connect the body paragraphs so that your discussion flows smoothly. Use some linking words and phrases like 'similarly' and 'on the other hand', though don't start every paragraph like this. Another strategy is to use a significant word from the last sentence of one paragraph in the first sentence of the next.

Use key terms from the topic – or synonyms for them – throughout, so the relevance of your discussion to the topic is always clear.

The conclusion ties everything together and finishes the essay. It includes strong statements that emphasise your central argument and provide a clear response to the topic.

Avoid simply restating the points made earlier in the essay – this will end on a very flat note and imply that you have run out of ideas and vocabulary. The conclusion is meant to be a logical extension of what you have written, not just a repetition or summary of it. Writing an effective conclusion can be a challenge. Try using these tips:

- Start by linking back to the final sentence of the second-last paragraph – this helps your writing to 'flow', rather than just leaping back to your main contention straight away.
- Use synonyms and expressions with equivalent meanings to vary your vocabulary. This allows you to reinforce your line of argument without being repetitive.
- When planning your essay, think of one or two broad statements or observations about the text's wider meaning. These should be related to the topic and your overall argument. Keep them for the conclusion, since they will give you something 'new' to say but still follow logically from your discussion. The introduction will be focused on the topic, but the conclusion can present a wider view of the text.

Essay topics

1. Lucy says to Lewis, "working with these people has changed you". Has Lewis really changed at the end of the play?
2. 'Each patient in *Così* has their own way of escaping reality.' Discuss.
3. Justin explains that the point of the play is to engage the patients and "bring them out of their shells". Do you think *Così Fan Tutte* achieves this?
4. '*Così* shows that love is a universal human experience.' Discuss.
5. 'In the process of rehearsing *Così Fan Tutte*, Lewis learns as much from the patients as they learn from him.' Discuss.

6 *'Così* draws parallels between madness and creativity.' Discuss.

7 Ruth claims, "comedy is better when it's real". How does this statement apply to *Così* itself?

8 *'Così* demonstrates how music can change lives.' Discuss.

9 Lewis tells Roy, "no one is a success or failure". How much does the play support or refute this statement?

10 *'Così* is a play about the triumph of fantasy over reality.' Discuss.

Vocabulary for writing on *Così*

Asylum: with few exceptions, this is how the characters refer to the mental institution where the play is set. While 'asylum' is a somewhat outdated phrase (reflecting the era of the play), and carries unsettling echoes of the politically incorrect phrase 'lunatic asylum', it also carries the connotations of refuge and protection: many of the characters in *Così* are seeking a refuge in the asylum from the 'real' world.

Black comedy: a theatrical form that juxtaposes morbid or sensitive issues with comedy.

Mad, madness: while it is difficult to discuss the play without these terms, Nowra is careful never to label the characters as mad (although sometimes other characters do: note that they are usually doing this in a provoking way). Certainly, other words used by characters as insults (such as 'loony') should not be used unless directly citing the text.

Naturalism: originally a theatrical movement in the late 19th to early 20th centuries, and with quite specific guidelines (covering content as well as style), naturalism has come to be used as a general term to describe a realistic style of writing/performance.

Opera buffa: Italian term for the style of comic opera of which *Così Fan Tutte* is an example.

Patient: this is the term Nowra uses in the play to refer to the residents in the institution, rather than 'inmate' or other terms that might imply a more distressing incarceration.

Socialism: a liberal political system that values social justice and equality among citizens. Lucy and Nick's political leanings tend towards socialism.

Analysing a sample topic

Lucy says to Lewis, "working with these people has changed you". Has Lewis really changed at the end of the play?

If the topic contains a quotation from the text, identify where the quotation is from, and be clear about the context surrounding it. Note the lines on either side of the quotation, and make sure you understand how this fits the overall structure and narrative of the play. Here, Lucy and Lewis are arguing, and it is at the end of this argument that Lewis says 'it's over. I'm shifting out of the house' (p.71). This particular line of Lucy's, then, is important because it is delivered at the height of the conflict between Lucy and Lewis, and foreshadows the final demise of their relationship.

Once you are clear on the meaning of the statement, you need to frame a contention. In the topic above, there are two alternatives: you can agree or disagree with Lucy's statement. (Or you could hover somewhere in between, but this can be much harder to do convincingly.) Often disagreeing with a topic or statement can be more interesting, but also more difficult. In this case, for instance, it would be possible to argue that in keeping with the genre of black comedy, the central character does not change throughout the play. However, there is evidence that Lewis has changed – if only subtly – so in this case it may be easier to agree with Lucy's statement, perhaps qualifying it by adding that the changes in Lewis' character are only small. For the topic above, then, your contention might be that 'working with the patients in the asylum subtly changes Lewis by the end of the play'.

Sample introduction

> Lewis begins *Così* as a character who is unsure of himself and has little confidence in his own abilities or in the task he is about to undertake. Nor is he secure in his romantic relationship or primary friendship. Through the process of rehearsing *Così Fan Tutte* with the patients in the asylum, Lewis learns to be firmer with his decisions, and to have confidence in his own skills. As a result, Lewis' personal relationships outside the asylum also change. He takes control of his life and makes decisions about his priorities, and although these are small steps towards his future, by the end of the play he has subtly changed.

Body paragraph 1

Identify examples from the beginning of the text which illustrate Lewis' lack of certainty, and rocky relationships:

- Lewis' first line, on entering the theatre, is 'don't know', closely followed by 'I need the money' and 'you said you were going to help me' – indicating his lack of confidence about working in the asylum.
- Although Nick and Lucy accompany Lewis to the theatre, they leave quickly and show no inclination to help him, indicating that their priorities differ from his, and he should not expect their support.
- When Lewis introduces himself to the patients, he is hesitant and his speech is halting, showing that he is nervous and uncertain.

Body paragraph 2

Examine the process of the rehearsals, and how Lewis' behaviour changes both towards the patients, and towards Nick and Lucy. Give examples:

- Lewis confidently stands up to Justin, lying to protect Doug and ensure that the opera can continue; not only is he committed to directing the opera but he later takes on Doug's role.
- When Lucy asks Lewis to decide between her and the opera, Lewis confidently chooses the opera and the patients, and equally confidently confronts her about her affair with Nick.
- Lewis confronts Nick about the affair, and about Nick's attitude towards the patients.

Body paragraph 3

Discuss how Lewis' behaviour has changed by the conclusion of the play, noting that these changes have been subtle:

- Lewis deals confidently with Doug when Doug confronts him after the opera.
- Lewis goes out on a limb, tentatively proposing an extension of the relationship with Julie (even though Julie rejects him).
- Lewis takes charge of his surroundings and at the very end of the play decisively turns out the lights.

Sample conclusion

Although Lewis does not manifest dramatic changes by the end of the opera, his final strong action – turning out the theatre lights – shows how confident he has become. He has broken up with Lucy and also written off his friendship with Nick, and these subtle changes are the result of his increased confidence, developed in the process of rehearsing the opera with the patients. Lewis has learnt new skills for managing people and for overcoming challenges, and it seems likely that he will be able to apply these skills in his life in the future.

SAMPLE ANSWER

'Each patient in *Così* has their own way of escaping reality.' Discuss.

Così is a play that is heavily concerned with illusion and reality. One of the ways it addresses this theme is to show how each patient's mental condition represents a way of escaping an otherwise stressful, upsetting or depressing life. The value this highlights is that it is possible to take control of your own reality and make life more bearable. As Zac says, 'I can't stand real things. If I could put up with reality I wouldn't be in here.' This could equally have been uttered by any of the other patients.

The patients, by living in the asylum, are taking refuge from the elements of reality that disturb them. Instead of facing up to, or enduring, the demands of society, the patients construct new worlds for themselves. They escape the 'reality' of life outside by creating their own realities within the asylum. This behaviour is generalised and shared by the patients. They all use this strategy but each has a specific and personal method for creating situations to escape from everyday life.

Julie, for example, 'can't imagine life without junk' – her drug habit is a way of transforming her existence. Her dependence is at such an extreme level that she can't imagine life without it, can't imagine living in 'reality' and chooses instead the world that drugs can create for her. Taking drugs is, for Julie, like being on 'a rocket to the stars' and it is her way of dealing with a world that is otherwise bland and meaningless, 'like being in limbo'. Julie's parents have committed her to the asylum, and, even though she does not like being there, her confinement gives her an opportunity to escape the reality of what her life on the outside has been. Being in the asylum also gives Julie the opportunity to take part in *Così*, and this becomes her new way of escaping – it gives her 'something' (other than drugs) 'to think about, something to do'.

For Roy, the opera has always been his way of creating a reality that is 'as far removed from this depressing asylum as possible'. The opera is more beautiful, more harmonious, more orderly, and more meaningful than the 'real' world for Roy, and it is part of a reality he has created for himself – the illusionary childhood he describes to Lewis. This is Roy's escape. The reason he wants to 'aim for the stars' and to convince others to do the same is that somewhere there, in among the 'music of the spheres' that is *Così Fan Tutte*, Roy believes there is a better life. He clings to this dream to avoid accepting the alternative: reality.

For Zac, as for Julie, it is drugs that make life bearable as they allow him to modify his own reality into a numbed, regular, predictable existence. As Julie observes, when Zac is on drugs, 'everything passes like a dream'. This suits him, and, when it comes time for him to design the set, although on a lower dose of medication, he is still keen to escape reality. His set design reflects his dreams and is a minimalist representation of the world – an escape from reality in its own way. Even when Zac eventually leaves the asylum, according to Lewis, he starts several rock bands, suggesting that maybe he is finding a new way to change his reality: instead of drugs, Zac's life is transformed by music. Music (presumably) replaces his heavy doses of medication and helps him escape the reality that he so loathes.

The other patients have similarly developed ways to escape their realities. Doug, on the opposite end of the emotional scale to Zac, wants his life to be as 'high' as possible, and creates his own exhilaration and stimulation, orchestrating situations of extreme danger by setting things alight. Henry has 'invented' (either consciously or subconsciously) the physical inhibition of his paralysed arm, perhaps to provide him with an excuse not to engage with a world that overwhelms and sometimes threatens him. Cherry invents a new reality where her unrequited love for Lewis is actually requited – she continues to act as though their relationship is a fact rather than an illusion, despite having received no encouragement from him. Ruth escapes reality by controlling it: by measuring it into numbered steps and regular patterns so that it becomes manageable.

These examples show how each character has their own preferred method for escaping reality and their own way of shaping life so that it becomes more bearable. All these behaviours and habits combine to contribute to the rehearsal and production of the opera – a collective escape from reality. In turn, the opera (the patients' escape from reality) becomes *Così*'s audience's own escape from reality. As we willingly suspend our disbelief for the time it takes to read or watch the play, we, like the patients, escape our own reality in favour of something more amusing, more entertaining, more beautiful and perhaps in some ways even more valuable.

REFERENCES & READING

Text

Nowra, Louis 1994, *Così*, Currency Press, Sydney.

Newspaper article

Bennie, Angela 1992, 'A comedy that fairly glows in the dark', *Sydney Morning Herald*, 23 April, p.16.

DVD

Così 1996, dir. Mark Joffe, Miramax. Starring Ben Mendelsohn, Barry Otto and Toni Collette.

Although the screenplay differs from the stage play, the film is still a useful companion to the text.

Websites

Bennett, Natalie 2008, *Theatre Review:* Così *at the White Bear, Kennington*, mylondonyourlondon.com/?p=187

IMDb.com 2009, *The Internet Movie Database*, www.imdb.com/

Nadarajah, Selma 2006, 'Così', *Sydney Stage*, www.sydneystage.com.au/content/view/104/

Tjhung, Mark 2009, 'Così', *Time Out: Hong Kong*, www.timeout.com.hk/stage/features/23151/review-cosi.html

Vaughan, Donna 2008, *The Papers of Louis Nowra*, www.nla.gov.au/pub/gateways/issues/93/story12.html

Other references

Brown, Bruce Allen 1995, *W.A. Mozart: Così Fan Tutte*, Cambridge University Press, Cambridge.

Kelly, Veronica 1998, *The Theatre of Louis Nowra*, Currency Press, Sydney.

Nowra, Louis 2004, *Shooting the Moon: A Memoir*, Picador, Sydney.

——1992, *Summer of the Aliens*, Currency Press, Sydney.

——1996, *Così: The Screenplay*, Currency Press, Sydney.

Reber, Arthur S. and Reber, Emily S. 2001, *Dictionary of Psychology*, Penguin, London.

Davidson, Jim 1983, 'Interview with Louis Nowra', in Jim Davidson, *Sideways from the Page: The Meanjin Interviews*, Fontana Books, Melbourne, pp.280–302.